Praise for

"Packed with expertise, wit, and actionable, useful information, *Free and Clear* gently and expertly guides you through the muck of being stuck into a better version of yourself.... Simply remarkable!"
—Kenneth Carter, PhD, ABPP, author of *Buzz!: Inside the Minds of Thrill-Seekers, Daredevils, and Adrenaline Junkies*

"The definitive guide to help you get unstuck and to avoid slipping back into the mud, *Free and Clear* should be at the top of everyone's reading list. Filled with relatable case studies, research-based evidence, and interviews with experts, this is a robust, inspiring book you can rely on when life's hiccups stop you in your tracks."
—Tammy Gooler Loeb, MBA, CPCC, author of *Work from the Inside Out: Break Through Nine Common Obstacles and Design a Career That Fulfills You*

"*Free and Clear* is the personal self-care resource we all need on our nightstand. Chock-full with meaningful information and guidance that will truly resonate with the reader seeking to get unstuck."
—Kathy Higgins, chief executive officer, Alliance for a Healthier Generation

"Shira Miller knows a lot about getting unstuck. If you feel like your life is on hold, read this book. It's well organized, upbeat, and filled with loads of great ideas to get yourself in the flow again."
—Lynn A. Robinson, author of *Divine Intuition: Your Inner Guide to Purpose, Peace, and Prosperity*

FREE
AND
CLEAR

FREE AND CLEAR

GET UNSTUCK AND LIVE THE LIFE YOU WANT

Shira Miller, CPCC

Copyright © 2022 by Shira Miller

22 23 24 25 26   5 4 3 2 1

All rights reserved. No part of this book may be reproduced, stored in a retrieval system or transmitted, in any form or by any means, without the prior written consent of the publisher.

Published and distributed by Shira Miller Media in Atlanta, GA
ShiraMiller.com

Library of Congress Control Number: 2022904382

ISBN 979-8-9857940-0-7 (paperback)
ISBN 979-8-9857940-1-4 (EPUB)

Editor: Jessica Easto
Cover and interior design: Morgan Krehbiel
Cover image: iStock/Vizerskaya
Author photograph: Daemon Baizan

Produced by Wonderwell
www.wonderwell.press

Printed and bound in the US

*For my mom, Faye Goldberg Miller,
who asked me to write a good book for her to read.*

CONTENTS

Introduction | 1

Part One: How You Got Stuck

CHAPTER 1: Realizing That You're Stuck | 7

CHAPTER 2: The 7 Things That Get People Stuck | 19

Part Two: Doing Your Homework

CHAPTER 3: Take a Pause and Quiet Your Mind | 47

CHAPTER 4: Find Your Purpose | 61

CHAPTER 5: Build Trust and Confidence in Yourself | 75

CHAPTER 6: Give Yourself Permission | 89

Part Three: Taking Action

CHAPTER 7: Become Resilient | 105

CHAPTER 8: Choose Positivity | 121

CHAPTER 9: Pivot with Purpose | 137

CHAPTER 10: Build a Support System | 149

Part Four: Maintaining Your New Trajectory

CHAPTER 11: Prioritize Wellness | 167

CHAPTER 12: Take Regular Internal Assessments | 183

CHAPTER 13: Practice Gratitude | 199

Conclusion | 211
Acknowledgments | 213
Resources | 215
Further Reading | 219
Endnotes | 221
About the Author | 230

INTRODUCTION

If you've picked up this book, you're feeling stuck in some area of your life. You're not living in alignment with your desired circumstances, goals, or purpose. You're beyond a short-term kind of stuck, like having a bad day at work or being late for an important meeting because of an intense traffic jam. Your "stuckness" has become a chronic state of being.

You've been living with it for a while now. It might be tied to a particular time in your life—like a milestone birthday or experiencing a midlife malaise—which causes you to second-guess major decisions. There may have been major disappointments with your love life and relationships with others. Or, you're feeling as if you keep letting yourself down when it comes to money, health, parenting, your career, or other areas. Even when you try to shake it off, that spiraling sense of being stuck inevitably comes back, like a boomerang, or shoulder pads as a recurring fashion trend.

And now you're ready to do something about it.

I wrote *Free and Clear: Get Unstuck and Live the Life You Want* for you—to help people who are ready to make lasting changes in order to break that cycle of stuckness and gain more meaning and fulfillment along the way. Perhaps you've put your family's needs above your own, and now it's time to finally start living for yourself. Or maybe you're facing one of the common yet challenging transitions of midlife—caring for children, helping aging parents, finding new love after dealing with divorce or death, or facing new circumstances with your health or body. The COVID-19 pandemic might have given you time to pause and reassess your life—maybe you want to quit your job or have already done so. This isn't a Band-Aid, a short-term fix with an expiration date. It's more like a lifestyle, a way of being. With this book, you'll learn a proven process for getting unstuck for good—and preventing future states of unfulfillment.

I am a certified professional co-active coach (CPCC), a two-time TEDx speaker, a writer focused on well-being, and the chief communications officer of a $2 billion corporation. My passion is helping people get unstuck and activate their full potential, probably because I've gotten stuck and unstuck so many times in my own life.

I've come to realize that my superpower—a special, unique set of skills that you will identify in yourself later on—involves a keen ability to overcome hard times and get unstuck, emerging stronger and happier than before. Over the past few decades, I've transitioned from financial ruin to prosperity, chronic health challenges to a constant state of wellness, obesity to sustaining a healthy weight, divorce to lasting love, and an unfulfilling career to a purpose-driven life.

I started to think critically about the moves I made each time it became apparent that I was stuck. It turned out that there were similarities, effective shifts, and specific tasks I could articulate as a step-by-step process. My curiosity was piqued, so I decided to conduct independent research to better understand which key factors hold people back overall. Over a three-year period, I interviewed more than one hundred individuals who overcame disruptions and intense challenges: like Marie, a jazz composer who completely burned out after holding her dream concert at Lincoln Center and had to recraft her purpose; and Suzanne, who moved to Sri Lanka to start a new business in midlife and found herself in an extreme COVID-19 lockdown; and Misty, who overcame a lifelong struggle with overeating by getting clear about her motivation.

Insights from these individuals proved to be illuminating. It became clear that certain patterns hold people back—time and time again—and that taking actionable steps can help all of us break free from undesirable situations. I realized that original research, dovetailed with my personal experience, created a body of knowledge that could help others get unstuck from whatever is holding them back. This book delineates that process to getting unstuck. You'll work through each step sequentially, chapter by chapter, building on the lessons learned to help you create positive, permanent change.

Part one is all about helping you understand how you got here—to your stuck place. You'll also learn the 7 Things That Get People Stuck and discover which pattern (or patterns) most applies to your own circumstances.

Part two covers what I call homework. You've identified what has made you stuck, and now it's time to do some heavy lifting. You'll learn how to cut through mental clutter to gain clarity on what you'd like to change, and set goals for your desired state of being. You'll gain more awareness about who you are as well as your purpose—especially as it may have shifted from an earlier phase of your life. You'll build greater self-trust by embracing your authentic self. And you'll grant yourself permission to change for good and avoid any self-sabotage.

All of that internal work prepares you for acting on the insights gained. That's why part three is about taking action. You'll learn how to become more resilient, face challenges head-on, and practice forgiveness. You'll discover how to choose positivity and strategically pivot when needed. And you'll build a healthy support system—or bolster the one you currently have—an often-overlooked part of getting unstuck.

Finally, part four concentrates on maintenance. You'll be on the unstuck path by now, and you'll want to stay there. People aren't perfect, and sometimes you may slip up. For example, a stress spike may cause the behaviors that got you stuck to reappear after you've banished them. This section helps you understand that a blip is not the end of your progress. You'll learn methods for preventing backslides and best practices to getting right back on track, such as prioritizing wellness to be your strongest self, gauging when things aren't solid, and practicing gratitude.

I'm so excited to see what lies ahead for you! Wherever you find yourself today—still relatively new to "adulting" and all it brings, actively reassessing your midlife circumstances, or considering how to build a lasting legacy—you deserve to get unstuck and live the best version of your life. Thank you for joining me on this journey. My hope is that where you stand right now will be a major turning point, bringing tremendous goodness into your world as you move forward.

Part One

How You Got Stuck

CHAPTER 1
Realizing That You're Stuck

I'VE ALWAYS BEEN fascinated by magicians. At a young age, I admired their ability to pull rabbits out of top hats or accurately predict which playing cards audience members would select. Elaborate costumes, spectacular stage sets, and dramatic music only made it that much better. But have you ever seen magicians who contort themselves into impossible physical situations, like tanks of waters with barely visible breathing tubes? It kind of freaks me out. I feel an empathetic wave of dread whenever I think about a magician choosing to be "buried alive" in a glass coffin for multiple days—or imprisoned in a box facing a huge buzz saw. Why would anyone deliberately choose close confinement, adding in handcuffs, cascading water, and more to increase the level of challenge?

On the one hand, it's a metaphor for being stuck at its worst. You don't have to be literally wrapped in chains to feel immobilized or out of options. Most of us can become just as trapped by run-of-the-mill life circumstances. For example:

> **An unfulfilling career.** Perhaps you're all grown up and still don't know what you want to do for a living. That string of jobs you've held is a means to an end because bills need to be paid.

You may have put a promising career on hold to raise a family or resigned along with millions of other people during or following the COVID-19 pandemic to reassess things, and you're now looking to make a comeback. Or maybe you got that manager, director, or executive title that you coveted, and though the compensation is good, what you do each day has become incredibly boring. Whatever the circumstances, your job or lack thereof does not fulfill the person you are today.

Financial struggles. The struggle to get by is real and is only getting worse. A steady income may be coming in, but it seems as if your student loans will never be paid off, or the cost of living in your area means that you can't save in the way you want to. Homeownership is something for others with greater means, not you. You might live paycheck to paycheck, having to decide between paying the rent or buying enough food to eat. Maybe you had savings at one point but then had to use it all for a medical emergency, and you now worry constantly about not making ends meet.

A midlife transition. Although life tends to shift for all of us at different points, women in particular experience multiple changes such as menopause, becoming empty nesters, caring for aging parents, dealing with ageism, and more—all of which can diminish your self-worth, increase your levels of frustration, and make you wonder when it will finally be time to start living for yourself after giving so much to others.

An unsatisfying personal life. This can take many forms. Your relationship sucks, but you stick around because of the kids or a fear of being alone—or you want to date someone great but can't seem to meet a person looking for the same kind of commitment you crave. Beyond romantic relationships, you may lament a lack of trustworthy friends or deeply miss spending time with your immediate family.

Being constantly at odds with your body. It doesn't matter what your doctor says. The number on your scale on any given day can wreck the rest of your week. You feel too fat or too thin, too short or too tall. Your hair, smile, complexion, or whatever is not what you want it to be. Picking yourself apart in the mirror or comparing yourself to influencers on social media is an exercise in self-defeat.

Health challenges. That new exercise routine you started at the beginning of the year evaporated following a sprained ankle. You've just been diagnosed with a heart murmur or suffer an unexpected heart attack. Whether you face a debilitating health condition or something that can be managed with a change in lifestyle or habits, it has you feeling down and out.

On the other hand, if you think about it, the magician is really a metaphor for getting yourself *unstuck*. After all, magicians are in control of the illusions they create. They aren't actually stuck because they're prepared, and they have strategies and skills for unsticking themselves. But unlike magicians, you don't always have a say in the challenges that life throws your way. However, you *can* prepare yourself with strategies that leverage your skills—even if you don't know what they are yet—to help you choose how to respond to those challenges and overcome them.

We'll get there. But for now, your circumstances are real—no illusion—and they're debilitating. I know what it feels like, having experienced it all.

What It Feels Like to Be Stuck

The feeling of being stuck is common. I define the term *stuck* as being at odds with your desired life circumstances. You don't live up to your expectations for yourself—whether that means in your job, love life, health, and more.

There are some kinds of stuck that, well, don't stick with you. A short-term kind of stuck. A dip in the road that can be easily overcome. Sometimes you might be having a bad day, week, or month where nothing is going right. An important meeting at work dropped off of your calendar, and you missed it. You were supposed to bring snacks to your kid's classroom and forgot. The cute dress you planned to wear to your high school reunion is too tight, and you didn't pack any other options. It can be completely out of your hands, like running into a major car pileup on the highway that causes you to miss a job interview.

None of these scenarios are ideal, but they will not derail you on a permanent basis. The funk quickly passes. You wake up one morning with the answer to a problem that has been bothering you or take a step to get out of a situation that no longer works. After a relatively short amount of time, you resume your intended course once more.

What we're going to focus on in this book is when stuckness becomes a chronic state of being. You've been living with it for a while, and even when you try to shake it off, that feeling of being trapped inevitably comes back. You've been in a stuck place for some time and are aware that there's a problem. But you might not be able to identify the cause specifically, and certainly don't know where to start when it comes to addressing it.

Not sure if you're chronically stuck or only stuck in the short term? In my experience, the sensation of being chronically stuck can take many forms:

You're wading through quicksand. You want to take a step forward or make a change but feel mired in place. You aren't really moving anywhere except downward into a spiral of more sand that is determined to wring the life out of you—and there isn't a spunky protagonist waiting to pull you out or a conveniently placed tree branch for you to grab. You're sinking down, down, down, and resisting just makes it worse.

It feels like you can't fully breathe. That's because you've gotten used to being in a state of fight, flight, or fear so long that you've been figuratively or literally holding your breath. You try to let air in, opening your mouth wide in an attempt to breathe deeply. It's not coming easily, though.

No matter what you do, it feels useless. Whatever actions you take feel ineffective. It seems as if you're doomed to repeat mistakes and missteps, never making a dent in the problematic situation. You can relate to the tragic figure of Sisyphus from Greek mythology, cursed for eternity to roll a huge boulder up a hill only to have it come rebounding backward when he approaches the top. It's a never-ending Groundhog Day of yuck, without the comedic movie patter.

You feel that you're out of options. You simply don't know what to do next, and it's terrifying. Making a single decision feels like it could have disastrous results. You feel helpless.

You experience constant disappointment. You aren't clinically depressed, but a cloud of disappointment is always hovering nearby. The college you dreamed about attending rejected you. That date you were excited about bombed. Your teenagers go out of their way to avoid spending time with you. After taking a new job on the basis of its supposedly great work culture, you found out a few days after starting that this wasn't the case at all. Nothing quite happens the way you want it to. Even when things go as planned, they don't provide the fulfillment you desire.

You're incapacitated by stress. Ever hear the phrase "Easy, peasy, lemon squeezy"? The counter to that is "Stressed, depressed, lemon zest." In this state, your stress levels are so high that it feels paralyzing. Anxiety is your constant companion. The stress is taking a toll on your wellness. You can't sleep.

It's hard to concentrate. With your stomach tied in knots, your appetite disappears, or you overeat everything in sight. There may be a constant temptation to self-medicate through an abundance of alcohol, cigarettes or weed, prescription drugs, or illegal substances—all because you feel so overwhelmed and are desperately seeking a break.

Any of these feelings sound familiar? I know them all too well. At the age of twenty-five, I had a quarter-life crisis. In classic overachiever mode, my midlife crisis arrived decades ahead of schedule.

On the surface, things seemed okay. I graduated from a respected university, scraping by with lots of financial aid, student loans, and working multiple jobs. I got a job in my field of choice, which was public relations. I had lots of friends and appeared to be the life of every party. The previous year, I married my first-ever boyfriend. But what many people didn't know was that I was experiencing nearly crippling self-doubt. It caused me to make some regrettable choices and adopt self-defeating behaviors.

For starters, I was fifty pounds above my natural weight. Ever hear of the Freshman 15? I doubled that in college with drinking and midnight-pizza deliveries. After graduation, an emotional-eating problem got out of hand. Many of my meals came from fast-food drive-throughs and the candy row of vending machines, even though I knew better. Although I had limited funds, that wasn't the issue. I kept reaching for processed, sugary treats for the temporary lift, creating a vicious cycle that left me constantly tired and sluggish. I looked and felt awful.

Also, my relationship was unsatisfying. Yes, marrying your first and only boyfriend may sound romantic. But at the time, I lacked the confidence and maturity to know that, though we loved each other, my husband and I had nothing in common, which would end up straining our relationship. He felt threatened by my career accomplishments, and I turned into a whiny martyr, trying to do things to please him while willfully ignoring my own well-being.

That career I was so proud of? It started crumbling. I adored my first job out of college, which was in the public relations department of a major US hotel chain. I had a great boss and liked my coworkers. I got the opportunity to create some innovative programs and won industry awards. That position became my primary source of self-esteem. Because I didn't want to go home and deal with an unfulfilling personal life, I became a full-fledged workaholic. Then, the job ended suddenly, following a corporate acquisition. I was offered a position with the new ownership, but I had no interest in moving nearly a thousand miles away. Despondent over that change, I took a role with a nonprofit, where the work environment couldn't have been more different. My job didn't seem to matter, which made me feel like *I* didn't either.

My lowest point took place in January of 1992. I cracked open a journal gifted to me by a friend and tried to list what made me feel good about myself. I stared at that page for what felt like hours before I came up with just one thing—my confidence in public speaking. Although many people fear speaking in public, I loved it. Competing in debate tournaments in high school changed my life. It was the first thing I had a true natural talent for that was totally mine. I excelled at speaking, and it made me feel special. Traveling around the country for tournaments, I started winning awards. I met peers who attended some of the most academically rigorous schools in the United States, which illuminated what was possible. It showed me that I could have a different and much bigger life. My success with speaking helped me get accepted into a great college and then, later on, stand out at work.

Acknowledging that talent created a sliver of hope. Maybe I could build on that one "pillar of strength," as I called it in my journal. Maybe I could use it to get unstuck and break out of that dark place that was holding me back. Maybe it could help me find my direction again, as it did when I was in high school.

That moment gave me the impetus to get help. I realized that it might be easier to get free and clear if I wasn't trying to do it alone. Although my friends and family cared about me, I recognized that an unbiased professional would offer me the best support. After a few tries, I found a wonderful therapist, started journaling about my thoughts and feelings, and on most days was buoyed by the initial breakthroughs that stemmed from writing. Those actions awakened a desire in me to treat myself like a friend—and I started empowering myself to reach for a more fulfilling life.

The point is, I get it. I've felt stuck, really deep-down stuck, several times in my life. Along the way, I wrote everything down, journaled about what worked and what didn't, then came back to revisit those practices with the benefit of hindsight. I pulled out those lessons learned and have applied them to myself when the going has gotten rough. I also taught them to the thousands of people I've coached, mentored, and addressed in presentations. I started sharing my insights in articles and talks. And I put those lessons in this book.

You are not alone—especially today, when global stress levels are on the rise. According to the Gallup Global Emotions 2021 report, the negative experience index score for 2020 reached its highest point in the survey's fifteen-year existence. That was during the height of COVID-19, before vaccines were available. The survey, which tracks participants in more than a hundred countries, found that 40 percent of adults had experienced worry or stress the previous day; that five-point increase represented nearly 190 million more people globally.

That sense of being stuck can extend to all parts of your life. Whether it's a dull sensation of being "off" or a pressing issue, you know when something isn't right. The problem is that most people don't know what to do about it. Then, something happens. It might feel awkward, surprising, awful, or wonderful—or even a combination of all those factors. The desire to tackle it, to live differently, is born. According to a December 2020 article in *Time* magazine,[1] the COVID-19 pandemic "caused a widespread existential crisis." Myriad challenges prompted people to reassess their lives and realize that another way was possible. I call this moment the "tipping point."

The Tipping Point

There are many names for it. The proverbial moment of truth. Coming to a crossroads. A watershed experience. I prefer the term *tipping point* to describe what happens when you have the idea to make a change, the strong desire to break free from what is holding you back.

In epidemiology (the branch of medical science dealing with the distribution, incidence, and control of disease in populations)—something we've unfortunately become too familiar with in recent times—a tipping point is the moment when a small change ends up shifting the balance of a situation and ultimately leads to a bigger change. In his fantastic book *The Tipping Point: How Little Things Can Make a Big Difference*, Malcolm Gladwell defines a tipping point as "the moment of critical mass, the threshold, the boiling point."

When it comes to being stuck, I've observed that the tipping point occurs when the pain of being stuck is less bearable than the effort needed to change circumstances. Just about everyone I interviewed in my research faced a tipping point of sorts. It might have been losing a job or not getting the one they dreamed about; ending a relationship, being diagnosed with an illness, coming home one night to find an eviction notice stapled to their front door, getting carjacked—the list goes on. Even a seemingly small incident can become the final straw after a series of disappointments.

For Emeka Nwosu, it was seeing two friends in their forties die from COVID-19. Previously, being uncertain about his purpose in life caused Nwosu to take a safe, proven career path instead of exploring areas that may have been more rewarding. He had a fancy title and a nice salary but felt overworked in a job that wasn't rewarding. Nwosu ignored his health, let his relationships slide, and didn't make time for the things he was passionate about, like travel and volunteering his time to help young people of color. Although he was dissatisfied, he wasn't motivated to get unstuck until the loss of those friends woke Nwosu up to his own mortality.

"For me as an African American, it became very real because the pandemic had a greater impact on minorities," Nwosu explained. "It made me wonder . . . if this were the last year I would be here, would I spend sixty-plus hours a week doing this type of work with my talents, energy, and effort, or maintaining the current relationships I've been maintaining? The answer was emphatically no. In many ways, it felt like I'd been sleepwalking through life just doing what I thought I was supposed to be doing as opposed to being intentional and purposeful around how I spend my time."

That tipping point caused Nwosu to make big changes. Prioritizing wellness, he began journaling, meditating, reading, and developing a financial plan that allowed him the freedom to pursue his passions. He quit his job within a year and spent a few months traveling internationally and exploring different cultures. Instead of putting himself under a tremendous amount of pressure to find one purpose, Nwosu started exploring multiple possibilities that will shift as he continues to grow.

Today, he is thriving personally and professionally. Nwosu took a fulfilling job that he enjoys, but he has created healthy boundaries with his time, and his relationships are flourishing. No longer stuck, he is happy and optimistic about the future while staying present in each day of his life.

As is evident in Nwosu's case, a personal tipping point occurs when you simply can't take your current circumstances anymore. The status quo is no longer acceptable. A realization—big or small—jolts you out of your inertia, dissatisfaction, or unhappiness and inspires you to get mobilized and do something about it. Getting unstuck resonates as a deep need that cannot be ignored.

Sure, the emotions you feel during that tipping point might be uncomfortable. No one particularly likes to sit in frustration, sadness, self-doubt, or anger. But within that, there's a kernel of hope. It might be minuscule, but it's there, telling you that a different way is possible. From that window of possibility, you can start to see and move toward a different way.

What It Takes to Make Lasting Change

You have the power to extricate yourself from whatever is holding you back. Everyone has that capacity, whether they realize it or not. I know you can actively say "I quit you"—whether it's to a person, behavior, or place—and get unstuck. There's no need to wait until you make it big as a TikTok star, win the lottery, or get an ultimatum from your doctor. Heck, you've already started the process by reading this chapter, so keep up the momentum! I'll be here along the way to provide guidance and cheer you on.

However, it's important to realize that the information in this book focuses on helping you make lasting change—it won't happen overnight. As you can see, getting unstuck is a process. Ensuring that you don't regress takes thought and planning. The first step is realizing that you're stuck, which you've already done. Then the next step is understanding how you got here. The upcoming chapter will help you identify your kind of stuck; then the groundwork starts in earnest. But following are a couple of things to keep in mind as you start your journey.

You can get unstuck no matter what you face. During my research, I interviewed people who experienced deep trauma, medical emergencies, financial ruin, heartbreak, and severe loss. For others, the circumstances were not as dramatic, but their kind of stuck—feeling hopeless, isolated, unworthy, lonely, lost, or at the end of their proverbial ropes—was just as stagnating. They figured out how to get unstuck without being, say, Olympic athletes, billionaire entrepreneurs, or teenagers who gained special powers after being bit by radioactive spiders. If they did it and I did it, you can, too. With determination, self-confidence, and a plan, anything is possible.

Getting unstuck doesn't have to involve drastic action. It takes time and measured steps forward to achieve your desired outcome. In fact, I don't recommend playing "go big or go home." Even when it looks like you're making dramatic changes or taking big leaps, a sequence of bite-size steps often proves to be more effective in the long term.

Engaging in a deliberate process helps make positive changes more permanent. There's a rhyme and reason to everything you see in this book. Yes, you're going to have to do some work, which will involve introspection, completing exercises to help develop new skills, and taking steps that aren't necessarily fun. But the payoff is huge. Keep thinking about the freedom you'll gain from surging past what was been holding you back; and how you care enough about yourself to reach for and achieve what your heart, head, and spirit desire.

Be patient, persistent, and stay the course.

You got this.

CHAPTER 2
The 7 Things That Get People Stuck

I'VE LONG WONDERED why people get stuck, and after three years interviewing more than a hundred individuals who overcame disruptions and intense challenges, I uncovered seven primary factors—attitudes, behaviors, tendencies, and ways of being and thinking—that get people stuck. The categories are somewhat broad, and they can take on many forms, depending on the individual. It's sort of like if your favorite ice cream flavor is chocolate, but the varieties range from rocky road to peanut butter chocolate to double fudge. They're related, but each one is distinct.

Right now, you know you're stuck in general, but you may not know what is *specifically* holding you back. This chapter will change that. Identifying which kind of stuck—or which *kinds* of stuck—you face is essential to breaking free. It will allow you to concentrate your efforts on the underlying problem and help you choose specific strategies to change the situation. In other words, *naming* your type of stuck gives you the focus and tools to permanently extricate yourself from self-defeating behaviors. My personal albatross is number four. Read on to learn about each one, then take the assessment at the end of this chapter to discover what your kind of stuck is.

1: You Don't Do You

Have you ever heard of the term *authentic self*? Your authentic self is the real you—the person who you truly are when you're being completely honest with yourself. It is your genuine personality without filters that hide perceived flaws, habits, or beliefs that might not fit in with your desired social group. Maybe you're brilliant at multiplayer video games, could happily eat ramen noodles each day, have an irrational hatred of farm animals, and haven't danced in public since that embarrassing incident in middle school. There's nothing wrong or right about these behaviors and thoughts; they're simply parts of the puzzle that come together to make you a unique individual. And when you eschew your authentic self for a self that is less than real, you may find that before too long, you're stuck.

"Being your true authentic self means that what you say in life aligns with your actions," said Jennifer Foust, an expert in family therapy and the clinical director at the Center for Growth. "Your authentic self goes beyond what you do for a living, what possessions you own, or who you are to someone (mom, brother, girlfriend). It is who you are at your deepest core. It is about being true to yourself through your thoughts, words, and actions, and having these three areas match each other."[1]

In other words, if you're introverted, you may be your authentic self when you choose to hang out with one or two close friends, and you may be inauthentic if you force yourself to go to a large party that doesn't actually appeal to you or pretend to be extroverted to fit in. It's possible to build an inauthentic persona either consciously or subconsciously. Either way, an intrinsic need to conform to social pressure might be the case.

According to psychotherapist and author Mel Schwartz, "We may disguise or manipulate features of our personality to better assure that others aren't judgmental or adversely reactive to us. If I worry about what others think of me, then I manipulate my personality and communication, either to seek approval or avoid disapproval. This masks my true or authentic self."[2] Inauthentic people may engage in behaviors such as "diplomacy, political correctness, false flattery, people-pleasing, avoidance, and silence."[3] Conversely, authentic people share their true selves openly—without filters—regardless of what the consequences might be.

In general, a fear of rejection frequently motivates inauthentic behavior. People often suppress their authenticity when they believe that "if you can't see the real me, then you can't hurt me." When I spoke to Kenneth Carter, PhD, a professor of psychology at Emory University, he agreed that avoiding rejection is a key element. Carter likens it to the concept of having a beautiful formal living room to impress guests and also a back room where the family actually congregates. "A lot of people protect their authentic self because they're afraid that others won't accept it," he noted. "They create this pretty, perfect, inauthentic front room for others to see because if people saw the rest of the house, they could be rejected. Having someone reject an inauthentic, false version isn't as damaging potentially as having the authentic *you* rejected."

Most people care what others think about them to some degree, but inauthentic people chronically compromise their true selves, which can start impacting their self-image and self-esteem. They may even forget how to be honest with themselves. The consequences are significant.

Being inauthentic creates a relentless amount of pressure to juggle who you're claiming to be with your real self. Wins feel short-lived because you worry that there will be a reckoning ahead. It can be mentally and physically draining[4] to sustain that facade. Research has also shown that being inauthentic can increase depression[5] and even feelings of being immoral.[6] In his book *Self Matters*, popular talk-show host Phil McGraw (Dr. Phil) notes that "forcing yourself to be someone you are not or stuffing down who you really are . . . will tax you so much that it will shorten your life by years and years." Plus, it's hard to build and sustain fulfilling relationships of any kind when you aren't creating them as your authentic self. For example, I loved a man who was really into the outdoors, and he ended up hiking the entire Appalachian Trail with his best friend. Although I liked nature in contained bursts, that was far from who I was in my early twenties. However, I went overboard in adopting his passions in order to deepen our connection; I would go on multiday camping trips or canoe over intense river rapids despite not enjoying those activities. Attempting to maintain that inauthentic behavior for several years was stressful and created a lot of resentment, ultimately contributing to our breakup.

When you're inauthentic, an undercurrent of fear is also always present. You're scared of being outed, of not being good enough, or being viewed as too much to handle. It's uncomfortable, like donning a jacket that's three sizes too tight but squeezing into it anyway because it matches what everybody else is wearing. It feels awkward and just plain wrong.

It can be surprisingly easy to be inauthentic, especially if you're driven by a desire to please others, as I was. Wanting to fulfill another person's goals for you—or what society at large deems appropriate goals—can feel a lot like desiring those goals for yourself. That was the case for one of my interviewees, Philippe Danielides. Growing up in a driven, educated, Greek American household strongly shaped his definition of success. His plan was to attend academically stellar schools and then become a highly compensated lawyer. Along the way, Danielides sometimes questioned if this was the right path. However, he ignored and suppressed his inner voice, feeling that it was just another challenge to overcome. The desire to conform to societal pressures or attain an ideal circumstance is a common reason why people veer off their authentic paths.

Danielides reached his career destination, as planned, by his late twenties, complete with a fancy place to live and a girlfriend. Unfortunately, it was a big letdown. He felt a sense of shame at being unsatisfied by his supposedly awesome life. "I was waiting to feel fulfilled, happy, and free, but it didn't come," he explained. "I thought other people's expectations and views of success were right, and that voice inside of me was wrong. I felt stuck because of the years spent actively distrusting myself, my instincts, my intuition, and my inner judgment about who I am and what I care about."

Other factors that prompt inauthenticity include feeling like you have to behave in a certain way to get ahead in business. This is a case of impostor syndrome, where you doubt your capabilities and feel that exposure could occur at any moment; and where you try to please or avoid disappointing others. Add in not having rock-solid self-esteem, which is true for many of us, and it's easy to fall into that behavior.

Bottom line: When you don't do you, then the best parts of you—the things that make you unique, different, special, and real—are denied or suppressed. You may lose your self-esteem and sense of direction and end up feeling lost or on an unrecognizable path.

2: You're on a Road to Nowhere

Your purpose in life is your reason for being. Everyone has one, whether they know what it is or not. After being shot by the Taliban for pursuing an education, Pakistani teenager Malala Yousafzai's purpose became helping all girls learn and lead. Apple founder Steve Jobs said that his purpose was to build an enduring company that prioritized people.

Sure, those are well-known examples. But you don't have to be an icon to achieve what brings you meaning. For my mom, her purpose was to be a loving parent. *Your* purpose might be ending a family cycle of addiction, planting a beautiful garden each spring, or living a life without regrets. Whatever the case, your purpose does not have to be grandiose or noble. It's what I call your "why," and when you find it, living in alignment with your purpose fills you with a sense of rightness.

However, many people don't know what their purpose is, or they don't live in alignment with it—they're on a road to nowhere—one that makes them feel aimless, untethered, confused, and frustrated. Without that vital compass to help navigate important decisions and circumstances, it's easy to become stuck. In your case, you may feel rudderless about where to live, how to develop healthy relationships, or how to deal with a growing pile of debt. "React first, think later" could be a bumper sticker on your car.

When you lack the tools to move in a meaningful direction, it's impossible to effectively chart your course and correct it when needed. You may experience something that researcher Larissa Rainey called "purpose anxiety" from not being able to identify your reason for being.[7] Purpose anxiety stems from craving a purpose and not being able to find it. You get anxious and frustrated during the search for your why, especially when comparing yourself to others who have seemingly found their way. The absence of, and search for, purpose can become a struggle at any age, which makes the road-to-nowhere experience of "stuckness" that much harder.

According to a July 2020 article on the Verywell Mind website, "Only around 25% of Americans adults cite having a clear sense of purpose about what makes their lives meaningful."[8] There are many reasons for that divergence. As mentioned earlier, social pressures to conform can cause you to listen to the voices of others above your own. When you aren't in touch with your authentic self, it becomes impossible to identify your true reason for being, much less honor it. You may lack self-trust and confidence, which we'll cover shortly, or you may have gotten caught up in external factors that make you unable or unwilling to look deep inside to find it.

Sometimes you may think you know your purpose and head off in a certain direction only to find that it no longer works for you. That's what happened to Marie Incontrera, whose lifelong purpose to be a concert pianist suddenly no longer made sense to her. As a child, Incontrera idolized Ludwig van Beethoven. She started playing piano at age five, mastered Beethoven's "Für Elise" at ten, and received a college degree in classical composition. After school, she started apprenticing with an opera composer and jazz musician who became her mentor.

It was a heady time, as Incontrera was learning jazz and playing alongside some of the best musicians in the world through her mentor's band. Terminally ill, he'd spent his life basically burning himself out for his art. After he died, Incontrera ended up starting her own jazz band, but she worked constantly and struggled financially, taking odd jobs in order to keep playing at night. "I lived in this tiny apartment and was broke," she explained. "Any money that I did make, or grants raised, were put back into that band."

Incontrera was scraping by on less than $15,000 a year in New York City, subsisting on ramen noodles to pay for her piano and apartment rental. She started doing virtual assistant and social media work on the side, using the extra funds to help raise $40,000 to pay for her band to play one night at Carnegie Hall in 2017. "We had a great concert, and it was one of the best nights of my life," said Incontrera. "But afterward, I didn't get out of bed for a week and knew something was wrong. I was completely exhausted from the excitement and fear of preparing for that concert and then finding there was literally nothing else on the other side." Incontrera was burned out, and sick and tired of putting her art before herself. She felt lost. The purpose she once had—to play jazz on a big stage—was no longer exciting to her or fulfilling.

It's not uncommon for people to pursue a goal or a dream—and when they achieve it, realize that they'd been ignoring the bigger picture of who they are in the process. When that happens, it's time to find a new way of life—one that allows you to craft a deeper purpose—or risk being stuck on a road to nowhere.

3: You Don't Consider Forgiveness

Like patience, wearing sunscreen, or always switching the lights off before leaving a room, forgiveness is considered a virtue. However, that doesn't mean it comes naturally for many of us. Being wronged in some way, intentionally or not, can get you stuck in a really negative place if you're unable or unwilling to work through those feelings. Often, we hold on to that energy, let it stew, and release it in damaging ways, such as anger, resentment, and revenge. And sometimes, the hardest person to forgive is yourself, even if you haven't done anything wrong.

According to the Greater Good Science Center at the University of California, Berkeley, "psychologists generally define forgiveness as a conscious, deliberate decision to release feelings of resentment or vengeance toward a person or group who has harmed you, regardless of whether they actually deserve your forgiveness."[9] In conducting research for this book, I found that an unwillingness to consider forgiveness can lead to a host of negative consequences. Some people I spoke with grappled with self-doubt, loneliness, resentment, or feelings of failure, while others felt paralyzed by the lack of resolution.

The Mayo Clinic notes that if a person is unforgiving, the consequences could include bringing bitterness and anger into relationships, an inability to enjoy the present, depression or anxiety, a lack of a greater sense of meaning or purpose, and the loss of valuable connections with others.[10] Let's look at three common types of unforgiveness that can get you stuck:

> **You committed a transgression and, while truly sorry, have not forgiven yourself.** Maybe you harmed a coworker's career by acting like a jerk, blew a tax refund on a gambling spree when you could barely make the rent, or cheated on a spouse. In all of those situations, you were at fault and deserved to apologize, make amends, or do whatever it took to right the wrong you created. You know that, and your regret is real. But out of a mix of frustration, embarrassment, and self-directed anger, you keep punishing yourself beyond a reasonable period of atonement.
>
> That's what Richard Bistrong faced. He had a high-flying career as the vice president of international sales for a large global manufacturer, traveling around the world selling products like armored vehicles and vests, riot control equipment, and

munitions to public officials and intermediary parties. Bistrong knew about a US law called the Foreign Corrupt Practices Act, which says you can't bribe a foreign official to either win or keep business. But after witnessing how commonplace bribery was in the international defense field, Bistrong rationalized it away, as he relished his luxurious lifestyle. Image was everything, and he developed a drug habit. Then in 2007, Bistrong was identified in a large United Nations bribery investigation. The former "golden boy" lost his job and became the target of a criminal investigation by the U.S. Department of Justice. His world came crashing down. Bistrong became an undercover co-operator, testifying at trials, and was ultimately sentenced to eighteen months of incarceration. Relationships with family members became strained or nonexistent. Although he'd been sober for years, the news coverage at his 2012 sentencing focused on his former decadent way of life. As Bistrong said, "It was just bad and ugly." He knew that amends needed to be made, but forgiving himself wasn't part of that initial process.

You've done nothing wrong, but you constantly beat yourself up. Let's say you go on a well-deserved vacation for the first time in years. An hour after reclining on that seashore hundreds of miles away, happily soaking up the sunshine, a text arrives that tears you to pieces—your mom just had a heart attack. You spring into action immediately, return home, and help care for her. After a period of convalescence, your mother heals. But it doesn't matter. Instead of being relieved, your primary emotion is anger—at yourself for not being present when a loved one was in crisis. That regret becomes so entrenched that you can't let go of it. You don't make time for yourself, much less another vacation. Anxious and fearful, you worry that something else bad will happen if you aren't focused on others all the time.

Or perhaps you've experienced personal trauma, such as physical, mental, or emotional abuse perpetrated by previous partners. You blamed yourself for not being supportive enough or for pushing their buttons or whatever line of bull they said prompted their unacceptable actions. Despite getting help and ending that cycle of abuse, you continue to kick yourself over the entire situation. Forgiving yourself—for being in that relationship, making excuses for the abuser's behavior, or taking "too long" to end it—is important. Otherwise, you can become trapped in a self-defeating cycle of shame that keeps you from fully healing.

When I spoke with Lisa Ferentz, LCSW-C DAPA, clinical social worker, educator, and president of The Ferentz Institute, she explained that "self-forgiveness is essential for healing because it's the antidote to the self-blame and shame that so many trauma survivors carry with them throughout their lives. When they're able to reach a place where they can let go of the ownership of their earlier traumatic experiences, really come to emotionally accept that what happened was not their fault and could not be prevented, they're set free and make this shift from shame to self-compassion."

Someone has hurt or wronged you. A man whom I'll call Ryan Lewis worked hard to build his upscale catering company into one of the most successful businesses of its kind within a major metropolitan area. Lewis promoted a charismatic employee into sales management, and their contracts continued to grow. Then the employee left to start his own venture, taking a huge chunk of clients and intellectual capital with him in the process. Lewis was devastated. Angry and hurt, he took it personally and spent the next decade focused on that betrayal—instead of looking at how to shore up the losses and regain market share. Yes, he was wronged. But an unwillingness to forgive the transgression and let go of the emotional angst around it festered a deep sense of resentment and bitterness. In the words of leadership expert Robin Sharma, "Forgiveness isn't approving what happened. It's choosing to rise above it."[11] Because he chose not to practice forgiveness, Lewis never bounced back professionally or personally.

The first two examples are about self-forgiveness. No matter where you might stand on the self-forgiveness spectrum—whether you've done something wrong or not—one thing is certain: practicing that kind of forgiveness is about self-compassion, and it helps rebuild your relationship with yourself. As psychologist and meditation expert Tara Brach said, "Feeling compassion for ourselves in no way releases us from responsibility for our actions. Rather, it releases us from the self-hatred that prevents us from responding to our life with clarity and balance."[12]

The last example is about forgiving others. To be clear, I don't believe we owe anybody forgiveness. The key word here is *owe*. Forgiving ourselves is necessary for our own well-being, but you do not have to extend that gift to someone who's done you harm. However, refusing to forgive someone can actually hold you back, as it did with Lewis, affecting your health, happiness, and more. For example, studies have shown that refusing to forgive can increase our blood pressure and other signs of stress.[13] It can also drive friendships and marriages apart.[14] This is true whether you're forgiving small violations or serious transgressions. Take the forgiveness research conducted by Fred Luskin, PhD, the author of *Forgive for Good: A Proven Prescription for Health and Happiness*, as an example. He applied his forgiveness therapy to individuals who've been through serious trauma—people affected by the violence in Northern Ireland and Sierra Leone, and US residents impacted by the events of September 11, 2001. His findings showed that those who went through general forgiveness therapy reduced their blood pressure levels, became more optimistic, and achieved greater peace with the past.

If you choose to forgive others because not doing so compromises your beliefs or keeps you from getting unstuck, that's another story. As you'll see in chapter 7, there are many strategies to learn how to forgive and gain greater resilience.

4: You Don't Trust Yourself

It can be difficult to trust others these days. When it comes to believing in yourself, though, that's another story. Not trusting your judgment and actions can lead to tremendous self-doubt, which is a one-way ticket to getting stuck. When you experience self-doubt, you question everything about yourself. Nothing feels good enough. Past relationships, your appearance, the clothes you wear, what you do for a living, your education, how you raised your children, and more are rehashed constantly in your mind into a singular, recurring verdict: you are lacking and useless.

Clinical psychologist Kristina Hallett, PhD, concurred when I interviewed her for this book. "One of the things that is so hard about not trusting yourself is that you become literally stuck in self-doubt," she said. "That's the bottom line. And when I think about self-doubt, I believe that is fully connected to the concept of feeling not good enough. If we took all of the problems in the world that people have, put them in a colander and strain them, what would be left is some version of 'I'm not good enough' at the core of everything."

Self-doubt can paralyze your ability to move forward, grow, or change, even when you know that those things might be necessary. Because you don't trust yourself to make good decisions, you stay within a narrow comfort zone of experiences and people. Risks are to be avoided at all costs, and even safe bets that may require a shift in habits fill you with apprehension. There's no sense of risk/reward; you avoid moments of growth out of a fear of failing the challenge.

When you don't trust yourself, this limits your self-awareness. Because you're filtering information about yourself through a "less than" lens, accurate messages about the state of things, the impact of your decisions, and more are not being received. It's like trying to fly an airplane with half of the engines turned off in the middle of a storm. This creates a broken system where you don't see the truth before you, and you trust the opinions of others more than you do your own.

Let's say you decided not to date a certain individual. During your first meetup at a restaurant, this person was overly critical, never asked you questions about your life, and was flat out rude to the server. It was a turn-off, and you ignored the text requesting another date—until a friend sees a photo of your date on an app, talks about this person's physical attractiveness, and complains about how hard it is to meet decent people at this stage of our lives. That buddy's comments cause you to second-guess your gut instincts. You decide to give this person another chance because of it, but then months later, you wonder why you're wasting your time dating someone who is obviously not right for you.

Personal distrust grows when you lack confidence, which often happens when people internalize negative feedback. A potential cause of self-doubt is how the most important individuals in your life react to your judgments and mistakes.[15] It can start at a young age, when people are just finding their way in the world. Research has shown that emerging adults who experience chronic self-doubt—which is reinforced by parents, caretakers, authority figures, and peers—can become overly focused on their imperfections and a fear of failure.[16] Maybe you dreamed about being the first person in your family to go to college and a parent said you lacked the necessary smarts, or schoolmates called you a loser for being in drama club instead of playing sports. Those trash-talkers were wrong, and you may know that now intellectually. But what remains is lingering doubt about yourself. No matter how successful you may appear to others, this sense of unworthiness can persist.

An example that comes to mind is Academy Award–winning actress Natalie Portman. Poised, eloquent, and beautiful, she appears to have it all together. However, when delivering the 2015 commencement speech at Harvard University, her alma mater, Portman let her insecurities show. She said, "So I have to admit that today, even twelve years after graduation, I'm still insecure about my own worthiness. I have to remind myself today, you are here for a reason. Today, I feel much like I did when I came to Harvard Yard as a freshman in 1999. . . . I felt like there had been some mistake—that I wasn't smart enough to be in this company, and that every time I opened my mouth, I would have to prove I wasn't just a dumb actress." Portman concluded her inspirational speech by urging graduates to carve their own paths in life. That glimpse of vulnerability shows how any of us can grapple with self-doubt, and it can have a lasting impact.

5: You're a Debbie Downer

Even if you've never watched an episode of *Saturday Night Live*, you might be familiar with the character Debbie Downer, created by comic Rachel Dratch. Debbie Downer could kill the mood at weddings, family reunions, and other joyous occasions by blurting out negative proclamations about feline AIDS, the mining of blood diamonds, mad cow disease, and more. Beyond satirical sketches, the truth is that we all know a Debbie Downer, a consistently pessimistic person who chooses to focus on the negative. It might even be you.

Do you ever fixate on one adverse comment after receiving an avalanche of praise, or find yourself consistently paying more attention to bad news over good? Unfortunately, a tendency to see the proverbial glass as not only half-empty but cracked isn't doing you any favors. My research has found that consistently choosing pessimism over optimism prevents people from overcoming obstacles and thriving.

Psychologists call exaggerated negative-thinking traps "cognitive distortions,"[17] a concept popularized and defined in the 1980s by David Burns, who is now a clinical professor emeritus of psychiatry and behavioral sciences at Stanford University. Some of them, such as "mental filtering" (sifting out all the positives to dwell on the negative) and "discounting the positive" (acknowledging but then dismissing the positive as worthless) are particularly indicative of Debbie Downers. Your brain actually tricks you into overestimating negative things and underestimating positive things—and you may or may not be aware of it.

Our tendency to gravitate toward the downside comes from a term psychologists call *negativity bias*. It means that most humans are hardwired to focus and respond to negative rather than positive stimuli, as it enables us to prepare for and avoid situations that may end badly. Way back in the day, when we had to be aware of foraging animals and other dangers, our fight-or-flight response played a key role in this tendency. According to Verywell Mind, the fight-or-flight response is "a physiological reaction that occurs when we are in the presence of something that is mentally or physically terrifying. The term 'fight-or-flight' represents the choices that our ancient ancestors had when faced with danger in their environment. They could either fight or flee. In either case, the physiological and psychological response to stress prepares the body to react to the danger."[18]

Today, we usually don't need that instinct to save us from a dangerous situation or negative outcome. But sometimes our brain doesn't get the message—it's still looking to protect us. When a fight-or-flight sensation sets in, spurring an avalanche of negative impulses and emotions, it's hard for some of us to think clearly. We may literally not be able to see a situation objectively or see how to get unstuck.

Additionally, fight-or-flight should be a form of short-term stress that resolves within a day or two. But if you're unable to shake your overall pessimism, you may find yourself with chronic stress, which can affect your physical and psychological health. According to Harvard Health, research suggests that long-term stress is associated with "high blood pressure; promotes the formation of artery-clogging deposits; and causes brain changes that may contribute to anxiety, depression, and addiction."[19] A 2016 study published in *BMC Public Health* found that being pessimistic can even increase your risk of death from heart disease.[20]

Being the pessimist can also impact your relationship with yourself and others. If you always point out what could and probably will go wrong in every circumstance, it sucks the joy out of everyone else's life—including your own. Determined to avoid disappointment, you can easily discount or avoid pursuing opportunities that may bring you joy. Predicting that the worst will happen makes sense in your mind, as it seems to protect you from an inevitable letdown. But because you don't reach for what you desire or take a chance to love, shine, trust, or grow, there's nothing positive to be let down from.

What causes a chronically negative mindset? Some experts suggest that it's a matter of both nature and nurture. The attitudes and behaviors of your caregivers may exert an immediate influence. If they frequently complain or see the world as being out to get them, you'll likely adopt those beliefs as well. When I spoke with life coach and family learning expert Susannah Chambers, she said that a nurtured negativity bias may manifest in infancy. "Research shows that when babies interact with parents, they respond to positive cues," Chambers explained. "By the age of three months, there's evidence that infants are already starting to interact differently based on negative cues."

Experiencing frequent disappointments in your formative years can create a pessimistic mindset. Bullying, the loss of a parent, poor living conditions, health challenges, and more can influence your perception, as you will tend to view the world around you as a punishing place. It can become natural to assume that the worst is yet to come. You may also gravitate toward negative thinking because it gives you an illusion of control when things feel chaotic. If you loudly predict that everything that could go wrong will, and that comes to fruition, you get to say "I told you so" and be correct.

In addition to distorted negative thinking, a Debbie Downer may also build oneself up by putting others down—just like a woman I know whom I'll call Karen Doe, who has lived her entire life feeling wronged. Since childhood, she has felt like the universe collectively cheated her out of better circumstances. Unhappy with herself but lacking the self-awareness to recognize it, she lashes out by actively insulting others. She delights in constantly pitting her three now-adult daughters against each other. On the day her youngest child got married, Karen made her burst into tears by saying that she looked fat in her wedding dress, and why couldn't she be more like her very fit eldest sister. Later that evening, while making a toast in front of hundreds of people, Karen made a snide comment about how her eldest daughter, the athletic one referenced above, was destined to be an old maid unlike her now-married sister. When her newly minted son-in-law left his job for a big promotion elsewhere, all she could talk about was how he never seemed to be able to keep a job for very long. Karen whines about not having any friends, but has driven people away for decades with her incessant negativity. As a result, her world is narrow, unhealthy, and lonely, because people avoid spending time with her whenever possible.

Unfortunately, being a Debbie Downer can become a self-fulfilling prophecy, and that's because a part of your brain called the reticular activating system brings whatever you're focusing on, positive or negative, to the forefront of your awareness. In the case of Karen Doe, she constantly anticipates the worst, such as not being invited to a social gathering in her neighborhood. Focusing on those negative possibilities makes her notice when it does happen, perpetuating her Debbie Downer cycle. As clinical psychologist Richard Shuster, PhD, explained during our conversation, "When we're having a bad time, we tend to focus on that. If we're dealing with adversity and what the potential negative outcomes may be, that's where our brain is going to be pulling data from in our environment to support that belief system. It can become a self-fulfilling prophecy, even if it's a transient stressor."

6: You're Not Flexible

When life throws you a curveball that requires change, do you make like Olympian Usain Bolt and run away at lightning speed? Do you bury your head in the sand or double-down into a spiral of denial? Hey, no judgment here. But as tempting as it may be, trying to hide from a truckload of change barreling your way is just going to get you run over.

That brings me to the pattern I call You're Not Flexible, which involves digging your heels into the ground when you're unwilling or unable to pivot when faced with changes, big or small.

This kind of inflexibility means that you refuse to change—even to your detriment. You risk losing out on professional opportunities, personal growth, and fulfillment. It harms your ability to be resilient—a concept that I'll talk a lot about in future chapters. *Psychology Today* defines *resilience* as "that ineffable quality that allows some people to be knocked down by life and come back stronger than ever."[21] Resilient people do not let "failure overcome them and drain their resolve, they find a way to rise from the ashes."[22]

There are other elements, such as adaptability and optimism, which can help make a person resilient, but I've found that inflexibility can completely shut down your ability to "bounce back," harming your well-being, relationships, and ability to thrive in many ways. Often, when it comes to getting stuck, those who fall into the inflexible category tend to wallow in being stuck instead of doing something about it, or they may feel they *can't* change or *shouldn't have to* change as required.

But the way I see it, you always have a choice. When I interviewed consultant, coach, and keynote speaker Dorie Clark, who was recognized as the number-one communications coach in the world by the Marshall Goldsmith Leading Global Coaches Awards, she agreed. "When circumstances change, you really have two choices," Clark explained. "One is to change and hopefully use it as an opportunity to get to an even better place to learn things and become more successful, or you stand still and shake your fist at the sky, which usually doesn't go very well."

Being psychologically inflexible can manifest in a few different ways. People may describe you as stubborn and set in your ways. You may be unwilling to consider different perspectives or behaviors, even when they make sense. Often, you may start sentences with the phrase "I can't/I don't/I won't" instead of looking at challenges with an open mind.

Fear lies at the heart of inflexibility, causing you to deny the reality of circumstances that may require a pivot. Change makes you uncomfortable because you associate it with a loss, whether that is a loss of power, control, independence, relevance, or a loss of who you are. Perhaps you've worked at a factory for twenty years and it's shutting down. Instead of figuring out how your skills apply to other roles or leveraging job-counseling resources, you feel that your skills are irrelevant and shut down, too.

This kind of stuck happens most frequently in three circumstances: (1) a change for the worse occurs, and people get overwhelmed and freeze up; (2) people are operating on autopilot and don't realize that they're stuck or can change; and (3) people do things that don't work but continue those ineffective responses based on how things "should be" versus how they are.

It's easy to understand these reactions to change, especially if those in question have spent a significant amount of time in pursuit of a pathway or goal that no longer works. It can feel that continuing on the same path is justified because of the time, resources, and effort that have already been applied to the path or goal in question. But that line of thinking describes a mistake in reasoning called the *sunk cost fallacy*.[23] It does not lead to good decision-making, nor does it negate the fact that your well-being is at stake when you don't adapt.

Not being flexible negatively impacts your wellness. The *Journal of Contextual Behavioral Science* found that "high psychological inflexibility was positively associated with the presence of stress, worry, generalized anxiety, and somatization."[24] A study of Japanese university students pinpointed a strong correlation between psychological inflexibility, increased depressive symptoms, and difficulty sleeping.[25]

Interestingly enough, you can be inflexible in one area but willing to roll with the punches in other ways. I've spoken to numerous people who found amazing success by pivoting in their careers but refuse to do the same when it comes to relationships or wellness. A woman I'll refer to as Gina Lopez comes to mind.

Gina wanted to meet the right guy. After college, she assumed that it would just be easy. Buddies would set her up on dates, and there would be numerous opportunities to "meet cute" at the dog park or in line at a coffee shop. But it didn't work out that way. True love connections proved to be elusive. Most of her friends met their significant others using apps or online dating sites and urged Gina to give it a try. Feeling that a soul mate would magically waltz into her life without any extra effort, she didn't want to do that. Her reluctance remained even though Gina knew statistically that most couples these days meet through online connections. Ironically, she has built a thriving career working in the information technology field that requires her to stay on top of industry trends. Now well into her forties without the romantic love she craves, Gina feels a dull sense of disappointment in her personal life.

Sometimes we all need to be more flexible—and resisting necessary change isn't just causing minor inconveniences when it leads to a chronic case of stuckness. (You'll learn more about how to adapt, pivot, and become resilient in chapters 7 and 9.)

7: You're Shipwrecked

Familiar with that movie-plot device of the "go it alone" hero—like the cowboy riding solitary into the sunset, the justice-seeking cop gunning a motorcycle on a deserted highway, or the superhero brooding in an underground cave after saving humanity once again? They didn't have to make it so hard on themselves. The truth is that most of us are better, happier, and smarter when connected with others. Even the Incredible Hulk, who tended to isolate himself from others because of his lack of impulse control, made great strides with anger management when teaming up with the rest of the Avengers.

A lack of connection with others, not being part of a supportive community, and an unwillingness to ask for help when needed is a tried-and-true recipe for getting stuck. I call this pattern You're Shipwrecked because you can feel isolated or lonely whether you're physically separated from people or living in a large city or household with others. It's easy to get trapped in your own thoughts, growing increasingly frustrated and negative. You don't have a network to run ideas by, help solve problems, or provide you with support.

When I talk about community, I mean like-minded souls. Birds of a feather. Your people, tribe, inner circle, amigos, clique, clan, homies, compadres. A *community* is technically defined as a social group where you share commonalities, but it can be a birth family or the family you create, such as people with common interests or practices, like a religious, educational, or civic group. The point is that you can create your community however you like. It might be specific groups for the short term or individuals who have your back throughout the course of your life. They truly care about you, and it is reciprocal; the mutual investment is real.

What matters is truly being there for each other. That sentiment is echoed by Lisa DeAngelis, PhD, of Dragonfly Coaching. During our discussion, she described community as "folks who are more invested in who you're becoming than who you've been. They're going to hold up the mirror to you, ask you the tough questions, pick you up and dust you off when you stumble, kick you in the butt when you're slacking, and be your biggest cheerleader. These are the people you trust, who'll be your truth tellers and have your best interests at heart."

In order to build a community, you need more than two people. Author and speaker Chris Guillebeau says that the threshold is three individuals, noting, "No man is an island, and two people can be a partnership, but you need at least three people to have community. Hopefully, over time you'll have more than three."[26]

Social isolation and loneliness are separate but related concepts. Social isolation occurs when you physically do not have many contacts. Loneliness occurs when the quality of your relationships is not at your desired level. Some people are happy being socially isolated, but for others, that isolation leads to loneliness, which is never a desired state of being. In other cases, people may have many social contacts but still feel lonely because the quality of those relationships doesn't match their needs or desires. You can have a million followers on social media, but if your interactions are just about likes, tepid DMs, or insults, that's about as fulfilling as eating potato chips and nothing else for dinner every night. It might sound fun at first, but it will eventually leave you with a sense of emptiness.

Social isolation and loneliness can hurt your well-being and mental health, too. The Centers for Disease Control and Prevention (CDC) reported that social isolation and loneliness can increase your risk of premature death, heart disease, stroke, and dementia; and lead to poor relationships, increased depression, anxiety, and suicide.[27]

Some people choose to go it alone, while others suddenly find themselves isolated or lonely. Why would you, for example, choose isolation? Several factors come into play: You may place a higher value on independence over connection. Sure, you pride yourself on being independent, whether that's by choice or circumstances. In the past, family or friends may have hurt you or let you down. You may associate being part of a community with weakness and being too vulnerable. This thinking may lead you to be unwilling to lean on others and accept help. It can happen even when you have a good network of people and you're always happy to help out your friends. However, you're reluctant to accept support, even when needed. It may be because you don't want to bother others, or you may feel that your needs are of lesser importance than someone else's. However, nurturing healthy connections is a two-way street. Not allowing others to give back support does you a disservice.

Also, you may find yourself isolated and lonely against your wishes. For example, you might move to a new city to take a job, but then it's harder than you realized to meet new friends. You have a major falling-out with your family, and they cut you off from all contact. After narrowing your world to focus on your romantic partner, the relationship suddenly ends. During the COVID-19 pandemic, loneliness became an epidemic when people were too scared to leave their homes for months or even years, so it's no surprise that undesired social isolation can hurt your well-being. According to GoodTherapy, "An isolated person may experience loneliness or low self-esteem. Over time, a person may develop social anxiety, depression, or other mental health concerns."[28]

You'll learn more about how to overcome this kind of stuck in subsequent chapters, where you'll develop your capacity to become more resilient and create positive support systems.

Assessment Tool: Which Type of Stuck Are You?

As you read through the 7 Things That Get You Stuck, I'm sure that some of the descriptors felt familiar. Now it's time to determine how you are *most* stuck in order to understand where to best focus your attention. Don't be surprised if you're stuck in multiple ways; this assessment tool helps pinpoint the area that you may want to concentrate on first.

For each statement below, please indicate which of the choices best describes you:

1. I don't often show who I really am.

1	2	3	4	5
Not at all like me	Not like me	Unsure or both	Like me	Very much like me

2. I don't know my purpose—my reason for being.

1	2	3	4	5
Not at all like me	Not like me	Unsure or both	Like me	Very much like me

3. I don't easily forgive myself or others.

1	2	3	4	5
Not at all like me	Not like me	Unsure or both	Like me	Very much like me

4. **I don't trust myself to make the best decisions.**

1	2	3	4	5
Not at all like me	Not like me	Unsure or both	Like me	Very much like me

5. **It's easier for me to be negative than positive.**

1	2	3	4	5
Not at all like me	Not like me	Unsure or both	Like me	Very much like me

6. **When things don't go as planned, I can't easily change.**

1	2	3	4	5
Not at all like me	Not like me	Unsure or both	Like me	Very much like me

7. **I don't have a community of support to turn to during good times and bad.**

1	2	3	4	5
Not at all like me	Not like me	Unsure or both	Like me	Very much like me

Tally up your total number below to determine your level of stuckness.

Overall Stuck Profile

0–15: Low threshold of being stuck. You may have one area in particular to focus on, but overall, you're in a good place.

16–27: Medium level of stuckness. There may be multiple areas where work is required to help you break free from whatever is holding you back.

28–35: High level of being stuck. You're seriously stuck in multiple areas.

Note each area where you scored yourself as a 4 or a 5. The diagnosis that each statement represents is listed below, so you can understand what types of stuck primarily apply to you. With that in mind, choose your highest-priority area for getting unstuck to tackle the tools throughout the rest of this book.

Statement 1: You Don't Do You—inauthentic, unwilling to show your true self

Statement 2: You're on a Road to Nowhere—unsure about your purpose and motivation

Statement 3: You Don't Consider Forgiveness—unwilling to forgive yourself or others

Statement 4: You Don't Trust Yourself—you grapple with self-doubt

Statement 5: You're a Debbie Downer—you actively choose pessimism over optimism

Statement 6: You're Not Flexible—you're unwilling or unable to change when needed

Statement 7: You're Shipwrecked—isolated, without a trusted community or support

Part Two

Doing Your Homework

CHAPTER 3

Take a Pause and Quiet Your Mind

IN THE PREVIOUS CHAPTER, you identified what kind of stuck best describes your circumstances. Now it's time to take a strategic pause to reconsider your life and the factors that are holding you back. In this chapter, you'll learn how to take a pause, identify the things in your life that you want to change, and determine what your desired future state looks like.

In today's 24/7 world, there's a lot of pressure to be wired and to be constantly on the go. It's not enough anymore to put in a full day's work and then enjoy life with loved ones. We're expected to document every moment on social media, know the latest news stories, juggle childcare, recycle as many household products as possible, and perform well at our jobs. Sometimes all the mental clutter can be overwhelming. That is why it's important to hit the "Pause" button and take a break from your routine.

Taking a strategic pause, which I define as any deliberate shift in your behavior to gain more insights, is an important step in getting unstuck. Doing so means that you're committed to supporting yourself. You care enough to try something different and look deep within. It doesn't matter if you're naturally an optimist or a pessimist. Some part of you—the part in the back of your mind that is leading the charge for change—knows that it's possible to have a more fulfilling life. A pause puts that voice in the driver's seat. Slowing down for a bit helps quiet your mind. When you get still and calm, even for a short while, a sense of openness unfolds. That fresh perspective allows you to identify the things in your life that you want to change as well as ruminate on your desired future state. You gain more confidence about your decisions and the road ahead. This chapter will help you learn how to do all of that and more.

What It Means to Take a Pause

As someone who is directionally impaired—which I don't think is an official term but certainly describes my lack of geographical acuity—I have a long history of getting lost on unfamiliar highways and surface streets. Being able to access satellite navigation systems has changed all that. These days, I don't leave home without consulting my GPS first to avoid traffic snafus and unexpected delays. It has made the trek to any destination much easier.

Engaging in a strategic pause at the beginning of getting unstuck is just like that. Before you start on your journey, you pause to decide where you're headed; then you activate your emotional and intuitive GPS to find the best route to get to your destination. It definitely beats aimlessly driving around and running out of fuel on the way, right? The kind of pause I'm talking about can take place over ten minutes, ten hours, ten days, or ten weeks—you define its parameters, depending on what you need and what your schedule can support. The most important thing is that your pause is intentional in nature. You are deliberately stopping in the moment to gain perspective and clarity. You are deliberately protecting that time and discouraging any interruptions. Honor the pause by turning your phone to "Do Not Disturb," shutting down digital devices, and avoiding distractions.

Your pause is about being introspective. During that time, you'll consider all the factors that contributed to your current stuckness and what your ideal situation could look like in the future. In the Take Action section at the end of this chapter, there is a series of questions and prompts to help guide you through this process of looking within. By the end, you'll be able to identify your desired state and general direction.

Setting goals for your pause is important. Let's say that the previous chapter revealed that you're a Debbie Downer. You can tell that your type of stuck is related to your financial situation—your tipping point was being denied a mortgage because of your credit score. Your first step is to consider what got you here, so you might explore your current relationship with money; what beliefs or fears contributed to the debt; your pessimistic viewpoint about your earning potential, spending habits, or the economy overall; and the factors (your actions and external circumstances) that led to your current less-than-stellar credit score. Then, based on this introspection, you'll identify the place you want to be and the changes that need to be made or actions that need to be taken to get there. Perhaps your desired state is to be a homeowner living in a place you love; and the things you need to change include your negative mindset, your credit-to-debt ratio, and your saving habits so that you can accumulate a bigger down payment.

Wondering where you take a pause? That location is up to you. Sure, it would be great to go out of town on vacation. If you have the means and time to do that, book it now! That's what Philippe Danielides, whom you met in the previous chapter, did. When the pain of staying trapped in an unfulfilling life became greater than the fear of leaping, he quit his job, got rid of his apartment, and bought a one-way ticket to Costa Rica to get in touch with his authentic self. That strategic, months-long pause helped Danielides look within and determine a new path as a professional coach. Today, he operates a successful coaching practice, helping unfulfilled high achievers grant themselves the permission to acknowledge and pursue the lives and careers they genuinely want.

However, you don't have to travel to another country. It can be as simple as changing your day-to-day scenery. Take a walk in a nearby park, or a neighborhood you've never visited, to gain a different perspective. Go to a coffee shop in another part of town. Ask a friend if you can borrow his or her place for the day. From the walls of your home, you could sit in a different seat, daydream in front of a window, or make a blanket fort to shift your viewpoint.

If you stay at home during your pause, think about decluttering that space. Research has shown that it's harder for your brain to remain focused when competing with multiple visual distractions,[1] and an abundance of clutter can lead to procrastination[2] and increased stress levels.[3] Trying to engage in deep thought at your remote work desk near the laundry room isn't going to cut it, especially when that pile of mismatched socks and unfolded towels begins calling your name. The same could be true for your favorite spot at the kitchen table, where you've got dirty dishes to clean, or a fridge full of snacks to distract you from looking within. Clean up whatever area you choose in advance so that physical clutter doesn't clog up your brain as well.

When we take a pause, one of the benefits is gaining a deeper connection to ourselves and the world around us. It helps counteract our typical overworked, oversubscribed lifestyles. According to "Conspicuous Consumption of Time: When Busyness and Lack of Leisure Time Become a Status Symbol," an article published in the June 2017 issue of the *Journal of Consumer Research*, a busy, overworked lifestyle has become an aspirational status symbol in the United States.

The study authors explained that "our investigation reveals that positive status inferences in response to long hours of work and lack of leisure time are mediated by the perceptions that busy individuals possess desired human capital characteristics (competence, ambition), leading them to be viewed as scarce and in demand.[4]"

That kind of thinking can create a lot of pressure to feel that you always need to be working or hustling in order to have value in our society. No wonder numerous people pack every moment of each day with so-called productive activities and meetings, leaving no time for introspection or simply breathing. Instead of giving ourselves time to just "be," we tend to gain validation by constantly having to "do"—to be productive and optimize each waking moment. "Being" refers to the state of simply existing—letting yourself be still, calm, and as good as you are in the moment, without rushing toward whatever the next "next" is, and without feeling that you're wasting time if you aren't moving and creating. *Being* is the opposite of the perpetual motion of *doing*.

Although each state is different, they're not mortal enemies. Having helpings of both being and doing on your plate can help unlock your full potential. However, when you *do* more than *be*, you reinforce your stuckness. Never pausing means you can't see a way out of that circumstance. You're on autopilot. You may be moving, but you're moving in a circle with blinders on—action without progress. Taking a strategic pause to assess where you stand today, at this moment, helps you take those blinders off and see beyond the circle.

If you don't pause to *be*, you will not only stay stuck but will eventually burn out—you know, that exhausted place where there's nothing left to give to yourself or others. Many of us have been there, and unfortunately, burnout is on the rise. In a 2021 survey conducted by Indeed.com, 52 percent of respondents said they were experiencing burnout. The most impacted group were millennials at 59 percent, up 6 percent from 2020. Gen Z reported a 58 percent burnout rate (up 11 percent from the previous year), and Gen Xers came in at 54 percent (a 14 percent increase). Baby boomers, more of whom are starting to think about retirement on the horizon, reported a 31 percent burnout rate (up 7 percent).

Burnout has become common precisely because we constantly *do* instead of giving ourselves time to *be*. It's like there's a mantra that plays on repeat, telling us that we aren't worthy unless the candle is burning at both ends. Everyone else appears to be optimizing their lives by working full-time jobs, launching side hustles, and becoming Instagram influencers all at once, so you should be doing that as well. It can feel overwhelming, without any sort of relief in sight.

Rachael O'Meara, the author of *Pause: Harnessing the Life-Changing Power of Giving Yourself a Break*, calls this concept the "pause paradox," explaining that people value the productivity and efficiencies of the world but don't give themselves permission to take any time off. At the heart of it lies a belief that you don't deserve to stop pushing. If you take a break, all of your efforts to be productive, be efficient, and achieve milestones become worthless. This is simply not true.

Living in a doing-based society can make it hard to access your ability to just be—especially when you get rewarded and recognized for being busy. But think about it this way: the state of *being* does not mean that you're *doing nothing*. Actually, you're actively listening to yourself and growing in that process. It takes effort to tap into being, but it is certainly worth it. And the benefits are numerous.

First of all, being helps you get in touch with your authentic self. Being allows you to live in greater alignment with your values and results in greater self-acceptance, trust, and inner peace. You can access your intuition more easily, and life feels more satisfying. Stepping outside of your busy life permits you to access your best self, brilliance, and personal power. The actions you take become more intentional. Relationships improve because you know more about yourself and what you need, and you recognize the kind of people who best support those factors. All in all, you communicate more clearly.

And the good news? Being has been a natural part of you since you entered this world. It may be hidden or suppressed, but you can learn to tap into it again. That's what life, leadership, and business coach Kacey Cardin confirmed during our discussion, noting that "your being is instantly accessible and always within you." On the other hand, doing is usually not accessible and therefore not achievable. "Doing is a constantly moving target," continued Cardin. "It's almost impossible to ever get to all the doing experiences on your list."

Case Study: Amy Burton Storey

Taking a romantic pause allowed Amy Burton Storey to figure out her previous stuckness and meet the love of her life. For years, she dated a string of guys who lacked the tools for healthy relationships, which proved to be frustrating. When she turned thirty-five years old, Amy decided to take a break from the dating merry-go-round and gain clarity with the help of therapy.

"I needed to pause, get sure-footing for my self-esteem, and become clear in my head about what I truly wanted," explained Amy. Her therapist helped pinpoint why she kept attracting the same kind of disappointing guys, allowing Amy to break that pattern. During that pause, the Louisiana native became clear that what she actually desired was a nice southern boy with similar values, someone who shared her love of reading, smart movies, and good conversation. With her newfound clarity, Amy recognized that this guy was Jason Storey.

They'd both dated others online for years without meeting the right person. When Amy reached out, she could tell that Jason seemed nice and honest, in addition to being attractive. On the first date, they clicked immediately. Jason quickly shared some past challenges that he'd overcome, and instead of running from it, as Amy might have done before therapy, she realized that Jason had the quality, confidence, and spiritual background she sought.

They got engaged eleven months later and have been happily married since February 2012. In August 2015, the Storeys expanded their family with the addition of their son, John.

Take Action

In this stage of getting unstuck, you'll take a strategic pause to gain insights on your situation and identify an overall goal for your desired state. Earlier, I explained what a pause looks like. Following are some specific actions you can take to effectively achieve the goals of your pause:

Action 1: Determine where you plan to take a pause. Will you go out of town or do this locally? Is this something that will take place outdoors or in your home? Consider weather, the people around you, and the potential for interruptions.

Action 2: Allot the desired amount of time. You're the only person who knows the best amount of time for your pause. If you're more contemplative or have a lot of thinking to do, several days or a week or more is terrific. Others who are already close to personal breakthroughs may need much less time. Scale your period of pausing accordingly, giving yourself the necessary time to achieve success within your busy life.

Action 3: Plan ahead. South Carolina patent attorney Tom Moses leaves home each summer to spend two weeks recharging in a remote fishing village in Alaska. He protects that pause by notifying clients, business partners, family, and friends months in advance about being unavailable during his absence. Even if you're planning a pause that lasts less than a day, planning ahead ensures that you get the most out of that shift. Make a list of everything that needs to be taken care of in your personal and professional life during that time so that you can delegate, reassign, get it done in advance, or push it off to another time.

Action 4: Quiet your mind. The best way to kick off your pause is to quiet your mind. Getting rid of constant internal chatter allows you to access wiser, more thoughtful parts of yourself. One way you might try to achieve this is through meditation.

According to the National Institutes of Health, practicing meditation may increase calmness and physical relaxation; improve psychological balance; enhance well-being; and reduce blood pressure, anxiety, depression, and insomnia.[5]

Sounds great, doesn't it? That said, I'm not particularly good at it. Some Zen-like people I know can meditate for an hour or longer, but my brain wanders shortly after getting started. If you tend to fall into my camp, try a five-minute meditation. Although claiming an hour for yourself may seem impossible, you can probably spare five minutes between waking and sleeping each day. I'm talking about time you already spend commuting to work, taking Zoom calls, or the moments before eating breakfast. Many smartphones allow you to download a free five-minute meditation app that clears your mind through guided breathing and imagery. Afterward, you might be surprised by how refreshed and focused you feel. You can also schedule an activity where being quiet is a prerequisite, like exercise. My fitness-loving husband does his best thinking and self-reflection during training rides, runs, or high-intensity exercise classes where checking his phone for messages isn't an option. You may also consider yoga, Pilates, or a stretching class to help you get centered and increase introspection.

Action 5: Look within. Jettisoning mental clutter makes you more open and receptive to answering important questions. I recommend recording your responses in writing or speaking them out loud into an app that lets you transcribe that information. Having these answers in written form allows you to reflect and refer back to them as needed. This step works best when you just blurt out your responses. They don't need to be pretty or sound perfect. Nobody is watching, unless you've invited a trusted friend or coach to undertake this process with you. Plus, you can always go back and adjust these responses as you get deeper into the process.

Go back to the kind of stuck you most identified with from the previous chapter. From that perspective, what isn't working in your life? List everything that comes to mind. What would you like to change? If your top unstuck factor came back as You're Shipwrecked, the list might include reaching out to friends, forming deeper relationships, asking for help when needed, and many other factors. After you write this out, circle the top two to three priorities, and then decide which should be at the top of your list. There's a reason why prioritizing tasks matters. Trying to do everything at once is overwhelming. It also doesn't work, as you can easily lose focus and momentum. Remember that this doesn't have to be a onetime activity. Years ago, I tackled my self-esteem first; then I moved on to prioritizing my physical health, building better relationships, and so on. Pinpoint the one thing you plan to change first, and then you can come back to address your next-highest priority.

Looking at your top priority for change, consider how this circumstance took place. What actions/inactions, beliefs, or thoughts of yours within the category of being isolated, for example, led you to being stuck in this area? Did you learn at a young age that getting too close to others might hurt you, or people would think you were weak if you shared challenges with friends? Who or what else contributed to your stuckness?

What does your ideal situation look like in this area in the future? Write down as much detail as possible, bringing it to life. Perhaps you want to move back to a smaller town where you can make a difference in your community, helping you refocus your energy after retirement. Think about how these circumstances make you feel (hopeful, joyful, content?), where you're located (in the city, the same place, a new place?), the people around you (old friends, new friends, family, other like-minded souls?), and more. Your answer here is your desired state.

Now it's time to identify an overall goal for your desired state. Think about the way you'd like things to be overall, regarding your relationship with yourself or other circumstances. In this ideal situation, consider what you'd like more of—things such as joy, freedom, achievement, or meaning—and what you'd like to discard—whether it be doubt, hardship, or loneliness. It must feel achievable so that you don't discount your goal.

Expressing this goal in a broad manner works best so you can avoid sweating out the minute details at this time. It could simply be "I have more energy," "I trust my decisions," "I seek adventure," or "My life flows smoothly." Going back to the Shipwrecked example, it could be: "I have meaningful relationships with others where we grow and support each other." With that in mind, you've just set your general direction. You'll know it feels right because now there's a sense of swimming *with* instead of *against* the current.

Exercise: Create a Vision Board

Now that you've taken that strategic pause and have identified your desired state, we're going to bring it to life through the process of visualization. Back in 2003, I led a workshop on visualization for a group of independent communications professionals. I brought crayons and paper with me, and after talking a bit about how creating a picture in one's mind's eye helps manifest something, I had everybody draw what they wanted to attract. One woman drew a picture of a house framed by beautiful flower boxes that she dreamed about buying one day, while another sketched an image of a diamond ring, since she wanted her commitment-shy boyfriend to settle down and propose.

Both concepts felt like pipe dreams to them for a number of reasons, but they created their images anyway. At the end of the workshop, I urged them to post their artwork in a prominent place in their respective living environments to serve as daily reminders of those goals. Fast-forward about eighteen months, and something interesting happened. The first woman hosted a dinner party, which I attended, to show off the new home she'd purchased. It was identical to the one she'd drawn, down to the flower boxes installed in the front windows. And when the second woman arrived, she was thrilled to share the news of her engagement and beautiful new ring.

Visualization helps us see what is possible in the future by giving our brains something to focus on and create over time. Seeing it is more than just believing it. The act of visualization allows us to tap into a more creative, resourceful perspective. It provides our minds with a place or concept on which to concentrate and then move forward.

This exercise teaches you how to create a vision board, a visual representation of the elements you'd like to create and attract into your life as part of your desired state. Here are the steps:

1. Determine your main vision-board theme with your desired state in mind. Craving better relationships with others? Consider how you'd like to portray this visually. Perhaps it involves finding images of happy romantic couples, friends hanging out together, people engaged in what looks like meaningful conversations, or a dining room table surrounded by a bustling family group.

2. Pick a medium. You can use thick poster board, or design something digitally to print out. Either way, you should have a physical memento when you're done. You can also make it three-dimensional if you like. One year I had an actual light bulb attached to my board to represent the eureka moment of creative inspiration.

3. Create your vision board. No artistic ability is required to draw, paint, or sculpt whatever will symbolize your vision; go crazy and repurpose things, if that's easier. Find images and decorative words or headlines online or in magazines, or recycle artwork from greeting cards. They should resonate deeply with you. Assemble your board in a manner that inspires and motivates you. I recommend saving the most influential message or image—the one that really reinforces your desired state—for the middle of the board. To make things "official," frame the board or slide it into a sheet protector.

4. Find a place for your vision board. Choose a spot where your vision board will inspire your journey of getting unstuck and thriving. I know people who keep it in home offices near their laptops, in their kitchens, and over their bedroom dressers, so they see it first thing when waking up each morning and before going to sleep at night. Take photos of your vision board to keep on your smart device so that you can refer to it while on the go. You may invite others into your journey, too, by sharing this image on your social media along with your desired, stated goal.

CHAPTER 4

Find Your Purpose

You've paused in order to quiet your mind and look deep inside. Feels good, doesn't it—to cut through the mental clutter and clearly see which factors contributed to your stuckness? In the previous chapter, you fleshed out and visualized your desired state (your ideal situation)—whether that pertains to your career, love life, health, or any other facet of life—and you've pinpointed one specific primary goal that you'll work on to help you get there. Now it's time to gain more awareness about who you are. This second step is all about finding your purpose.

There's a distinct difference between your desired state and your purpose. Building on where you want to be, which is the goal for your desired state, your purpose is something much deeper and motivational.

Simply put, your purpose in life is your reason for being. It's an intention to accomplish something that matters to you. I refer to your purpose as your *why*, the force that motivates you. I've always liked that term because it reminds me of children asking why-type questions to start learning more about the world around them. Persistent curiosity and an openness to discovery is vital to development—both children's and adults'.

To really get a handle on your purpose, we're going to explore different facets of your identity. That includes asking yourself powerful questions to understand your why and your values. You'll become aware of what you want and your desired impact on the world at large. You'll identify your natural talents and strengths so that you can put those assets to work in achieving the positive vision you hold for yourself. All of these factors will allow you to best accept and support yourself in this journey to self-awareness.

What It Means to Find Your Purpose

Everybody has a purpose in life. It's the reason why we're here, the impetus for our existence and meaning. However, that doesn't mean that people are *aware* of their purpose.

As Jack Canfield, the bestselling author of the Chicken Soup for the Soul series, has noted, "We are all born with a deep and meaningful purpose that we have to discover. Your purpose is not something you need to make up; it's already there. You have to uncover it in order to create the life you want."[1]

Unfortunately, we don't come into this world with an instruction manual. Certain lucky individuals figure out their whys at a young age. For others, they may come later, and some may never look inside deep enough to identify them. Sometimes we just get so bogged down by life and the expectations of others that our whys are hard to see. Even when our purpose is crystal clear, we can still lose our mojo and momentum along the way. When we don't know our paths or diverge from them, it becomes easy to get stuck in a rut.

Wherever you currently stand on that spectrum of self-awareness, knowing your purpose brings all sorts of good into your life. Think winning season tickets to watch your favorite sports team or getting a selfie with your celebrity crush is great? Well, that pales in comparison to realizing your purpose. Doing so provides the baseline you need to stay on, or return to, the path you desire. It serves as a yardstick to measure how things are unfolding. There's a sense of surety and confidence. Even when situations don't go as planned, you feel good about your general direction. Meaning is apparent, even in the midst of chaos. You can do more and be more because your goals are so clear. Living on purpose gives you more fulfillment. As bestselling author and speaker Simon Sinek wrote in *Together Is Better: A Little Book of Inspiration*, "Most of us live our lives by accident—we live as it happens. Fulfillment comes when we live our lives on purpose."

Understanding your purpose starts with knowing yourself: becoming honest about who you are, being willing to evolve, and developing a keen sense of self-awareness pays off in numerous ways. For starters, gaining this kind of awareness can promote your personal and professional growth.

Caroline Stokes, a certified executive coach and the author of *Elephants Before Unicorns: Emotionally Intelligent HR Strategies to Save Your Company*, has seen numerous individuals flourish after gaining more self-awareness. "Self-awareness is hugely important since when you know who you are, when you know what is holding you back or what areas you need to develop, you're going to succeed," she told me. "You can admit mistakes and learn from them. Your verbal communication, body language, perspective, and behaviors become more effective, attractive, and endearing to others."

Having a strong sense of purpose can also improve your health—and even extend your life expectancy. A 2019 study published in the American Medical Association's JAMA Network Open found that having a purpose in life can help people live longer.[2] Longevity expert and bestselling author Dan Buettner has discovered similar results. He has studied "blue zones," places across the globe where people have the greatest life expectancy. Buettner found that one of the commonalities shared by people who live more than one hundred years is possessing a keen sense of purpose.[3]

Then there's the benefit of reducing the risk of disease. Alan Rozanski, MD, a professor of medicine at the Icahn School of Medicine at Mount Sinai in New York City, has focused his research on the relationship between life purpose and physical health. In a 2015 article he published in the journal *Psychosomatic Medicine*, Rozanski noted that having a strong life purpose was associated with decreased incidents of cardiovascular events, such as heart attacks and strokes, while also reducing the risk of mortality.[4] Other researchers have found that individuals who have a lower sense of life purpose were 2.4 times more likely to develop Alzheimer's compared with people who reported a strong sense of purpose.[5]

Gaining awareness about your values—the principles, beliefs, and ideals that guide your behavior—can help you find your purpose, as does understanding your natural talents and strengths, because these may reflect what ignites your passion and joy. (In the Take Action section, you'll see steps to gain more knowledge about both of these concepts.)

Interestingly, your purpose isn't typically fixed in place, like a GPS coordinate. As you grow and change, it can evolve as well. However, be mindful that sometimes it can feel like you're being driven by purpose when the motivating factor is actually ego or the perception of others. A sense of purpose is purer than that; it is your true why and should not be dependent on others for validation.

That was certainly my own experience. When I was in my twenties, I didn't know to look deeper, so I defined my purpose solely through the filter of career aspirations. Back then, I decided that the key to happiness was becoming a vice president of a big company by the time I was thirty-two. That oddly specific goal was completely based on ego and how others defined a successful career path. Ironically, I did get offered that very opportunity at that exact age and turned it down because I'd outgrown it as my purpose started to become clearer to me.

In my thirties and early forties, my purpose had evolved into using my powers of communication for good: representing great companies and people I believed in, influencing organizations to explore corporate social responsibility programs, and more opportunities that could make the world a better place. Still, I continued to place too much emphasis on what others thought. I racked up awards, had a PR firm with my name on the door, and occupied a fancy office space—yes, all of the common status symbols. Until the Great Recession of 2009 brought it all crashing down.

By my fiftieth birthday, I'd learned to follow my inner compass over the voices of others. It was a relief to trust and listen to myself, getting clear about what mattered most rather than muddying the waters by relying so much on external approval. Before, I'd used my communication skills to promote and amplify positive developments. Like eating oatmeal or flossing daily, it felt like the "right" thing to do and helped validate my sense of accomplishment and worth. Today, my purpose is to help people get unstuck and activate their full potential. I'm not motivated by ego strokes or looking good in the eyes of others, as I was previously. When I live my purpose through mentoring, coaching, and speaking, it fills me with a burst of happiness. Seeing others realize that they can make positive life changes and achieve their goals is extremely fulfilling—and is one of the reasons why I wrote this book.

Cue whatever inspirational music may be playing at the back of your mind right now; I hear the dulcet tones of the *Chariots of Fire* theme song. Over the span of thirty years, my purpose has evolved from being about me to encompassing "we"; and today my purpose is about meaning, passion, and making a difference way beyond myself. The point is that it took me a long time to find my purpose, and without that inner compass, I wasn't headed in the right direction. When I shifted my initial purpose from myself to the community at large, it became more meaningful. In his book *The Path to Purpose: Helping Our Children Find Their Calling in Life*, Stanford psychologist William Damon defined *purpose* as having three parts—being larger than day-to-day objectives; reaching in some way beyond yourself; and including an achievement, progress, or completion.[6]

Bottom line: knowing your *why* is critical to finding your *what*. If *why* is your purpose, then *what* is how you deliver on that each day. I really dig how comedian Michael Jr. explains it in his popular *Know Your Why* video: "The key isn't to know what, the key is to know why. Because when you know your why, you have options on what your what can be. Your what has more impact because you are walking toward your purpose." Michael Jr. says that his personal why is to inspire people to walk in purpose, while his what—the way in which he brings that mission to life—is through performing stand-up comedy, writing books, creating web series, and more.

In other words, finding your why helps you choose a what—and acting on that what to fulfill your why is what gets you unstuck. Career and executive coach Tammy Gooler Loeb agreed when I asked her about this topic. "It's important to know what motivates you and around which values you're operating your life, because that's what's going to get you unstuck," she said. "It's at your core, where you feel the most grounded. You find your why from a place within yourself, regardless of what is going on in the world around you. When you know your why, the what comes so much more easily."

Case Study: Patrice Tanaka

Finding her purpose was the last thing on Patrice Tanaka's mind when she sought help from an executive coach in February 2002. Like other residents of New York, she continued to reel from the September 11 terrorist attacks that had occurred five months earlier. Patrice was exhausted from caring for her husband, who'd been fighting a long battle with a brain tumor, and the challenges of building her public relations agency, PT&Co., with twelve partners. Many days, it was hard to get out of bed in the morning.

During their first session, Patrice was surprised when her coach asked her to rethink her purpose in life. It proved to be a challenging assignment. As Patrice considered possible purpose statements, she couldn't stop thinking about the thousands of people who'd died in the Twin Towers attack. "The moments before you know that you're going to die, I would want to believe that I'd done what was most important,"

she told me. "But like most of us, those individuals were banking on living long enough to do the things that mattered most, and they just ran out of time. I wanted a purpose where I would never be in danger of that. So I told my coach that my purpose was just simply to choose joy in my life every day, to be mindful of that joy, and to share that joy with others."

Finding her purpose changed everything for Patrice. She started exploring what brought her joy in the past, and her love of dancing topped that list. As an eight-year-old, her dream was to dance like Ginger Rogers, but in all of the decades that passed, she'd never taken a dance lesson. Prodded by her coach, Patrice signed up for lessons. It was awkward at first, but soon she was hooked. Patrice began competing in ballroom-dancing competitions locally, then nationally and internationally, winning championships along the way. It was a joyous experience that opened up her world; dancing became Patrice's *what* to help her practice her *why* of choosing and sharing joy.

Patrice wrote a book called *Becoming Ginger Rogers: How Ballroom Dancing Made Me a Happier Woman, a Better Partner, and a Smarter CEO*. The lessons she learned from ballroom dancing helped her thrive professionally. In 2015, she departed the public relations world to create Joyful Planet, LLC, to help build purpose-driven individuals and organizations.

"While most people agree that a life purpose is important, they just don't place a great sense of urgency around it," Patrice said. "But research shows that having a life purpose helps people live longer and enjoy healthier relationships while equipping us with a competitive advantage that can focus and drive us to accomplish what matters most."

Case Study: Misty Boachie

Knowing her why has proved to be transformative for Misty Boachie multiple times. In the first instance, doing so helped Misty overcome a lifelong struggle with overeating. During childhood, she had no boundaries set on what to eat, or how much. By sixth grade, she weighed 250 pounds. Misty lost one hundred of those pounds in middle school, but then the weight crept back on throughout her twenties. When she was pregnant with her last son at age thirty-five, the scales topped 270 pounds.

Misty was done with the yo-yo eating habits, lack of energy, and being constantly worried if clothes would fit. What really changed, though, was her why—an intense desire to be able to keep up with her kids and to create a good legacy for her children's health. In order to do that, she had to learn how to eat better and embrace exercise. The extra pounds came off, she improved her body image, and being fit and healthy became her norm.

Misty's purpose to set a healthy example for her children continued to expand during the early 2020s in the atmosphere of increasing racial unrest. A Black woman, she began her own personal outreach program by calling friends who are not people of color to engage in honest conversations about race relations. "I felt called to action on a deep spiritual level, to share more of myself and my personal experiences with racism, the fears that I have for myself and my family, and also to invite others to talk through these issues and work through them together," she said. As a result, Misty says that she's become more courageous, steadfast, and expressive, which encourages her children to do so as well.

Take Action

Gaining self-awareness is essential in finding your purpose. But how do you do that? Using the desired state you identified in the last chapter as an overall guidepost, take the following steps to discover your why:

Action 1: Chart your Wheel of Life. The Wheel of Life is a simple, easy-to-use diagram that allows a person to pinpoint, on a scale of 1 to 10, what their level of satisfaction is with different areas—health, career, family life, relationships, and more. (You can download a sample Wheel of Life chart from my website.) The first time I saw this diagram and filled it out back in 2013, my pattern looked like a sunburst with rays of high scores in relationships and travel and low scores in career and finances.

Be honest with yourself when you complete the chart, as it provides important data points about what is missing in your personal and professional life. Think about why your scores are low in certain areas and what you can do to gain more satisfaction and self-knowledge. Then use those insights to plot your course moving forward.

Action 2: Answer thought-provoking questions. There are two ways to proceed with this step—answer questions on your own, or have a trusted resource pose them to you. I recommend writing your responses in a journal or a computer file, or speaking them into a recording app. But if that sounds about as fun as a root canal, consider partnering with a friend or a professional, such as a coach or therapist, to help with this process. Here's a starter list of questions to use on your own or with a partner. Add in whatever else pops into your mind along the way:

> What matters most to you?
> What are your must-haves in life?
> What do you take pride in?
> What are you most passionate about?

What would you like your legacy to be?
What have you lost that you'd like to regain?
What do you wish you had more of?

Action 3: Define your values. As mentioned earlier, values are the beliefs that guide your behavior and represent who you are at your core—things like adventure, kindness, courage, and honesty. (You can find a grid of values in the Resources section of this book and at ShiraMiller.com.) As you review the answers to questions completed in the last step, circle the values most aligned with those insights. Now narrow it down to your top-five values.

Action 4: Understand your strengths. There are a number of assessment tools like Values in Action and Clifton Strengths-Finder that can help you identify and cultivate your natural talents. I recommend that you take a few of them. What you learn about yourself may be surprising. For example, I assumed that empathy might be one of my top skills, but one assessment scored me higher on being imaginative, futuristic, and strategic. Another assessment that focused on overall character traits identified my top traits as "creating" and "valuing close relationships with others." A friend of mine learned that an appreciation of beauty tops his list. Identifying these values will help you engage with them later on.

Action 5: Identify your passions. Unlike a hobby where you might have an enduring or passing interest, a passion incites a strong, positive emotion within. Consider what really motivates and excites you, and make a list. Look at those items and circle the two or three passions that resonate most deeply with you. For example, perhaps you've had a lifelong love of sports that brings you joy, or you feel strongly about volunteering with at-risk kids because after-school programs kept you from getting into trouble while growing up.

Action 6: Go back to your peak experiences. Look back at a time—it could be a minute or a whole year—when everything felt just right. Think about what your life circumstances were and why that time was important to you. Pinpoint a few examples of when you felt the most grounded, had a greater sense of connection, or solved big problems or achieved a personal milestone. What kind of impact were you able to have, or what impact did that have on you?

Action 7: Actively seek feedback. Think about who you trust in your personal and professional life. Asking these individuals to provide you with honest feedback about a circumstance, behavior, or decision allows you to grow and improve. Just be fully open to receiving the insights you requested. You might not like what you hear. But uncomfortable truths need to be received so you can realize the reality of situations and get unstuck for good.

Action 8: Brainstorm your purpose. Using all of the outputs you've created, brainstorm what your purpose might be. Remember Marie Incontrera from chapter 2, the jazz composer whose purpose no longer worked for her? She realized that her values included creating art and inspiring others, while two of her natural talents were bringing people together and identifying unique hooks and selling points—and that leveraging what she was doing with social media brand-building to fund her artistic ventures allowed her to make a bigger, more meaningful impact overall. Today, with that understanding, Incontrera defines her purpose as helping others discover their greatness and put it out into the world, while doing the same in her own life and work. "Now my business affords me control over my life while I can pursue artistic projects that I feel good about," said Incontrera.

Let's say that when thinking about your peak experiences, you realized that the happiest time in your life was raising your children. It wasn't just because you adored your own offspring; it was gratifying every time you volunteered to read in their kindergarten classrooms and see all of the kids get excited about hearing stories and using their imagination. With that in mind, your purpose might be to encourage children to love to learn. That could take shape in many ways, from becoming a schoolteacher, volunteering to help young kids learn how to read, working part-time at a day care, and more. Or, when considering what you take pride in, it could be your talent for bringing people together in a harmonious way. Your family members might be full of drama and petty grudges, but when they come to your home, suddenly everyone gets along because of the planning you've put into every part of the experience.

Make a list of what your purpose could be, discuss it with others if needed, and see what speaks to you the most. It doesn't have to sound pretty or perfect; this is just about identifying possibilities. Cull down the list and then move on to the following exercise.

Exercise: How to Write a Statement of Purpose

A statement of purpose is a simple, clear description of what your purpose is and how you can accomplish it. Typically one or two lines long, it cuts to the heart of your reason for being. There's a lot of power in articulating your purpose in this manner and reinforcing it to yourself and the world at large. Declaring this intention makes it real and official and can lead to scrutiny from others, if you're open to it. Use your desired goal from chapter 3 and the outputs from the Take Action section—such as your values, passions, strengths, and purpose—to complete these steps and craft a statement of purpose.

Make it simple. Coming up with a short, easy-to-remember phrase will keep you focused. Here are a couple of templates to consider in reflecting your goal. Pick one you like, tweak it however you desire, and fill in the blanks:

> My purpose is _____, and I do this by _____.
>
> I am here to _____, and I deliver this by _____.
>
> Because my purpose is _____, I _____.

Examples of completed purpose statements include:

> *My purpose is to be a great parent, and I do that by raising kids who make good decisions.*
>
> *I am here to help people enjoy financial freedom, and I do so by sharing my wealth management expertise.*
>
> *Because my purpose is to make the world a better place, I volunteer my time with nonprofits that fight cancer.*

Make your statement of purpose accurate and achievable. Stretching yourself is great. Perhaps you'll be the first person in your family to go to college because you've seen how it can create more opportunities. In that case, your statement might be: "My purpose is to inspire others to expand what's possible through education, and I do so by getting a master's degree and volunteering with Big Brothers/Big Sisters." That's excellent, and obtainable with work and dedication. However, choosing something completely out of the realm of possibility where you don't have the potential aptitude or ability might become an exercise in futility.

Your purpose should also be inspiring. Choose a statement that makes you want to reach for more and allows room for growth and development. Let's use this example: "Because my purpose is to make the world a better place, I volunteer my time with nonprofits that fight cancer." Making the world a better place is an open concept that allows you to adjust the delivery of it however you like. Volunteering time at nonprofits is something that is within your grasp, while something like "I will *cure* cancer" is likely not realistic.

Make your statement of purpose bigger than just you. When your purpose statement has been finalized, here are a few more steps to get the most out of it:

Add resonance. The more positive energy you pour into reinforcing your purpose, the more powerful and achievable it will become. Repeat it out loud to yourself frequently. Write down where you currently stand in delivering on your purpose. Visually reinforce your purpose with an object or screensaver image to keep it top of mind. Years ago, when I was focusing completely on work and not much else, I bought a simple ring comprised of two interlocking pieces—one was gold and the other was silver. The gold symbolized my personal life, while the silver meant career to me. Then I'd flip which side would be on the top side of the ring while I wore it depending upon my need to balance different factors. Starting a day leading with the gold side reminded me to prioritize my well-being and time with friends and family members; then I flipped it back to silver when dealing with intense deadlines and major work-production needs. After a few months, I didn't need that talisman anymore, but it definitely was effective in reinforcing my intention.

Use the statement as a litmus test. Plan to check in on your purpose statement weekly, monthly, or even daily to ensure that your thoughts and actions are aligned with your overall mission. Share it with some trusted individuals, or blurt it out to the world. Making it a colorful banner on your social media site can serve as positive reinforcement.

CHAPTER 5
Build Trust and Confidence in Yourself

IN THE PREVIOUS CHAPTER, you gained awareness about your values, strengths and, ultimately, your purpose—they're all there laid out before you. However, not trusting or believing in yourself will hold you back from applying those insights.

It's like seeing an amazing dessert—let's say carrot cake because that's my personal favorite—prepared on a popular cooking show. After tracking down the recipe, you spend hours painstakingly chopping nuts, grating carrots, sifting flour, and more before mixing it all by hand. But then, right before placing the concoction in the oven, you hesitate. You wonder if it will live up to the hype of the professional chef-crafted cake, worry if your dinner guests will enjoy it, and start second-guessing whether or not you measured everything correctly ("Did I use salt instead of sugar?"). Meanwhile, that batter sits sadly in its greased cake tins on the counter, slowly curdling. It doesn't matter how great that cake might have tasted because you never end up baking it, which is both a waste of your time and the cake ingredients.

The point is that this stage of getting unstuck relies on building your internal reservoir of self-trust and confidence. It doesn't matter how many smarts you have if they're underutilized because you lack the confidence to move forward. You may have had confidence in spades in the past and a disappointment knocked you off your game. Perhaps you possess it in one area but not in the ways needed to pull yourself past the obstacle before you. This chapter is all about how to counter that in order to get unstuck for good.

What It Means to Build Trust and Confidence

When you trust yourself, the counsel you seek above all others is your own. You feel confident about your decisions and are willing to take risks. Even when desired outcomes don't manifest, it doesn't matter. You know that you'll figure it all out and rise up again. That's because your belief in yourself is strong. In an increasingly uncertain world, you're sure of yourself. And that kind of self-confidence is a powerful predicator of success.

Bestselling author James Clear summed it up well in his book *Atomic Habits*: "The biggest difference I've noticed between successful people and unsuccessful people isn't intelligence or opportunity or resources. It's the belief that they can make their goals happen. When I've discovered an opportunity that sounds awesome but that I'm not qualified for (which happens often), I trust that I'll figure it out and go for it anyway. I believe in myself. This confidence has made the difference for me again and again. I didn't need intelligence or opportunity or resources. Just a simple belief in myself."

In other words, self-confidence is a feeling of trust in your abilities, qualities, and judgment. This concept is often confused with self-esteem, which is about *valuing* yourself—different from *trusting* yourself. Then there's *self-efficacy*, a term coined by psychologist Albert Bandura, which is your belief that you *can execute* a specific task. These concepts are related because self-confidence (or lack thereof) can impact all of these areas. If you don't trust your qualities or judgment, you may not be able to see your value either. And if you doubt your abilities, you may diminish your chances of success. When your self-confidence grows, so does your self-esteem and your self-efficacy. You trust your decision-making and your ability to complete necessary actions and tasks—all of which helps you break free from challenging circumstances and move toward fulfilling your purpose.

Self-confidence truly is the linchpin. In *The Self-Confidence Workbook: A Guide to Overcoming Self-Doubt and Improving Self-Esteem*, coauthor Barbara Markway noted that "self-confidence is linked to almost every element involved in a happy and fulfilling life," including less fear and anxiety, greater motivation, more resilience, improved relationships, and a stronger sense of yourself.

Embracing your authentic self is one of the most impactful steps you can take to build self-trust and confidence. I'm talking about the real you, with all of your quirks, gifts, goofiness, and more that is sometimes kept under wraps in order to fit in or avoid rejection (see You Don't Do You in chapter 2), which is often a contributing factor when people get stuck. Practicing authenticity leads to greater self-acceptance. You live in alignment with your values and beliefs. Being true to yourself grounds you in reality. Your capacity to count on yourself, to truly show up and be present, expands.

That's not all. As reported in a January 2002 article called "The role of authenticity in healthy psychological functioning and subjective well-being," researchers asked a group of nearly eighty psychology students at a large southeast US university to complete a sixty-item Authenticity Inventory and other measures. That study found strong correlations between authenticity and more self-esteem, life satisfaction, and a sense of well-being.[1] Hopefully, none of this is surprising to you. Consider how you feel when living in authenticity. Perhaps there's a sense of freedom or greater ease, resulting from the removal of inauthentic behaviors.

One way to be authentic is to be honest and speak your truth. Let's say that you just started dating a longtime crush who is super adventurous—I'm talking about rock-climbing steep ascents and spelunking into some pretty scary-looking caves. You, on the other hand, get nervous when scaling a standard household ladder above the middle rungs. You try to like the activities your partner does and engage in many of them, but it makes you miserable. Rather than pretend to adore these activities as much as this person does, be real about it. Define how and when you'll participate in a manner that could be more fun to you, or let these activities be things your partner enjoys alone or with friends while you do your own thing. You might be nervous about having that conversation, wondering why your love interest never seems to catch the subtle hints of eye rolls or white-knuckle grabs as you cling to a rock cliff for dear life. But once the discussion takes place, chances are good that you'll feel a sense of relief. You're choosing to be your authentic self, which is vital in order to build a strong longer-term relationship—with yourself as well as your partner. Remember that it's normal and healthy to ask for what you need in a relationship. Not seeing eye-to-eye with respect to certain activities doesn't mean that you can't compromise or have a fulfilling relationship overall with someone who has different interests. And if you being you ends the relationship, then it wasn't on particularly strong ground to start with.

Another way to build self-confidence and trust is to lean into the strengths and talents you identified in chapter 4. Let's say that one of your strengths is tenacity. You've leveraged that determination in so many ways—working multiple part-time jobs to put yourself through college, moving past a difficult divorce, and caring for a child with special needs. Think about how tenacity has helped you overcome challenges that someone else may not have been able to handle. Acknowledge how that gift makes you capable, different, and special, allowing it to fill your well of confidence.

At times, I had to remind myself of my own strengths—perseverance and optimism among them—as I wrote this book. I stopped and started this project for years, putting it on the shelf whenever my full-time corporate job got too busy. Then I resumed in earnest in 2018, interviewing and researching and developing the 7 Things That Get People Stuck that you read about in chapter 2. The first draft was nearly completed in 2020 when the COVID-19 pandemic struck. I paused, not sure what the world was going to look like during those unprecedented times. Then I decided to pivot, reframing the book around getting one's mojo back when the pandemic ended. And then, after completing that new version in the spring of 2021, my publisher said that this different thrust would limit the impact of the book, which kept it frozen in time as society moved forward. Sure, I knew that advice was spot-on, but hearing it was still overwhelming. Faced with the need to rewrite much of this book, I was filled with intense self-doubt. Yes, the author writing the book on getting unstuck got crazy stuck herself while bringing it to life in this incarnation! Talk about #irony.

However, several things—besides working with a great editor—helped me persevere. I went back to my purpose of helping others get unstuck and activate their amazing potential. I reviewed all of the articles I'd published on this and related topics—about a hundred at that point—which served as my personal proof that I could execute the rewrite. Reflecting on everything I'd accomplished against the odds throughout my life reminded me of my determination and increased my self-confidence. Recognizing my unique viewpoint as a certified executive coach—who'd lived so many aspects of getting unstuck herself—made me more determined to share my knowledge. It didn't matter anymore if the people buying this book just consisted of my mom's mahjong group and a smattering of friends. When I became focused on my purpose and my strengths, I bolstered my confidence with the exact process I'm recommending that you take in this chapter, and I started to mobilize.

Letting yourself be vulnerable is an important facet of authenticity—and it's difficult to be vulnerable if you lack self-trust. Society tends to celebrate those who are strong, tough, and display grit. But trying to live up to that standard can make it harder to be vulnerable, since some people view vulnerability as weakness. However, displaying vulnerability is necessary to grow and thrive—and I believe that it's a sign of strength, not weakness. Admitting that you're having a difficult time takes self-trust. It means being confident enough in yourself to see that, even if you're in a low place or are making some mistakes right now, you won't be there forever because you have the ability to evolve. That takes a tremendous amount of strength, as does asking others for help. It improves relationships and helps you heal.

In her insightful bestseller *Daring Greatly: How the Courage to Be Vulnerable Transforms the Way We Live, Love, Parent, and Lead*, Brené Brown draws upon more than a decade of research to show that vulnerability is actually the best measurement of personal courage. "When we shut ourselves off from vulnerability," she wrote, "we distance ourselves from the experiences that bring purpose and meaning to our lives."

Vulnerability is not only a sign of strength and courage; it is an essential component in getting unstuck. Jon DeWaal, the executive director and life transition guide at Liminal Space, a nonprofit organization in Edmonds, Washington, sees tremendous value in being vulnerable. "Until we share the vulnerability of what we're going through," he told me, "I don't think it's possible to get unstuck, discover what you need, or see how you're going to bless the world around you. Everyone wants a sense of purpose—a way of understanding how we fit in this world. Vulnerability is the path to get us there. Vulnerability is the invitation to share what we'd rather guard and protect: stories of pain, loss, disappointment, and shame. What gives vulnerability its core power is the act of sharing our lives with others. It is a relational word; and you will not discover the substrate of you, create meaningful connections to others, and build a purposeful future without it."

Case Study: Deborah Carter McCoy

Over the past few years, Deborah Carter McCoy has learned how to trust her own instincts. It didn't come naturally, though—mainly because she spent decades second-guessing herself and putting the needs of others first, a behavior that diminished her self-confidence.

Deborah had built a full life in St. Paul, Minnesota, raising two sons with her husband; playing on an ice hockey team; volunteering in a variety of leadership roles; and working with a county government to build public awareness about economic growth, public transit, and environmental issues. She always had huge career aspirations but placed them on the back burner to take care of her family. However, with the children now grown and her husband well established in his own business, Deborah decided that it was time to think about doing something bigger.

She cast a wide net, exploring new career possibilities throughout the region. To her delight, she was offered a leadership role with an influential policy, planning, and communications firm in Chicago. The job offered much of what her heart desired—the chance to lead major initiatives, help manage the firm, and mentor emerging talent. It seemed perfect. With the full support of her husband, Deborah took the leap. She rented an apartment in Chicago, created a commuting situation that worked for her marriage, and gave it her all.

It should have been time for a victory lap, but then cracks became apparent in the new company's culture. Much of what she was promised did not materialize. The negative work environment became oppressive, and Deborah started to plan an exit strategy, only to lose her job. All the high hopes she once had for the experience were gone. It caused Deborah to significantly question her own judgment. She was filled with self-doubt about everything.

"When people demean you, make assumptions, or dismiss you

because you don't fit the mold they want for you, the emotional toll can be significant," she told me. "The move and professional opportunity held so much promise, and when it did not work out, I felt unsettled—unmoored, really. How did I go from being a well-respected, high-performing professional to someone so easily discarded?"

Deborah launched a consultancy and immediately landed clients, but she struggled to regain trust in herself after that big disappointment. After mourning the loss, she started building self-confidence by getting in touch with her authentic self. She read voraciously and sat with her thoughts and feelings. Meditation and gratitude lists also helped, as did leaning into her spirituality. Going deep within to reflect on her identity and values, Deborah sought to understand her life experiences. That journey of self-exploration taught her a lot. She was able to recognize the positive impact of her personal and professional efforts, which proved to be an eye-opening, positive exercise. Without realizing it, Deborah simultaneously strengthened her self-confidence, self-esteem, and self-efficacy.

"I've always been a risk taker, but I haven't always trusted my instincts," she said. "Going through long-unopened boxes and reading my recent reflections, I noted that my contributions to the communities in which I've lived, worked, and volunteered have made lasting changes and are valued by others."

Deborah moved back to St. Paul full-time. Armed with greater self-trust, she started considering new ways to make a difference in the world. She became the director of strategic communications for a leading environmental nonprofit organization; and her work has helped transform how businesses, nonprofits, and the community come together to deal with environmental challenges on a global scale. Today, she is thriving professionally and personally, and her ability to trust herself has never been stronger.

Take Action

Trusting yourself is essential in order to get unstuck. Being authentic by remembering your purpose and leaning into your strengths and values will help develop your confidence muscles, preparing you to continue this process. Try the following steps to maximize your trust and belief in yourself:

Action 1: Practice self-compassion. Have you found that constantly beating yourself up and second-guessing decisions seems to make everything worse? It's time to bring on some self-compassion, which involves being honest yet kind with yourself when assessing a circumstance.

Start by choosing a specific situation from your life. For example, let's say that you've been diagnosed as morbidly obese. Your doctor is worried about recent blood-work results that point to the potential for heart disease or diabetes. Since learning this news weeks ago, you've been racked with fear and self-loathing, berating yourself for damaging your own health.

Take a deep breath and write down the circumstance in detail, on a screen or paper. Then let it sit for a couple of hours or days; the intent is to create distance between the situation and your harsh self-judgment.

Now think about your best friend (here, let's refer to her as a female)—you know, the person who always has your back no matter what. What would she say if you were sharing this circumstance with her? As a supportive pal, I'm assuming she would listen intently and express confidence that you can make the desired changes with a different approach. Going back to your write-up about the circumstance, add that kind of response to yourself. Leading with thoughtfulness instead of withering criticism, be understanding in acknowledging your fears. Reinforce your positive qualities, and express why you know that you'll claim better health, just as your friend would.

Action 2: Continue the kindness. Check in on yourself on a weekly basis. Give yourself kudos for progress and a compassionate reality check when needed. Point out what you've done right while committing to changing what isn't working. Recognize that no one is perfect and that you're only harming yourself by trying to live by an impossible standard. It's all about striking a balance in the way you regard yourself, and ensuring that no matter what happens, self-love is present. The ability to completely trust yourself is only going to come when you can be self-compassionate. Seeing yourself in that more balanced, positive, and honest light helps diminish internal criticism, something we're going to tackle further in chapter 6.

Action 3: Create a reverse bucket list. A bucket list (as in "kicking the bucket") contains the things you wish to experience before dying. In a reverse bucket list, you list those things you've already accomplished to serve as irrefutable evidence of your commitment to yourself. Listing these items reinforces that when you have a goal, you can be trusted to accomplish it. For example, you might feel stuck about how to handle an excessive amount of credit card debt. Rather than berate yourself for not handling your finances well, which just creates a sense of shame without solving the problem, consider what you *have* achieved. Did you graduate from college? Organize a successful fundraiser for your child's school? Learn how to swim after being terrified of water? These achievements all serve as proof of your talents and skills. Taking a third-party perspective—like a benevolent yet emotionally uninvolved bystander glancing at your life—can help. List everything that comes to mind, and jot down a few notes about how each accomplishment makes you feel. This step builds confidence and boosts your self-efficacy, reinforcing that if you were able to crush those other tasks, you can get unstuck with credit card debt or whatever challenge is top of mind right now.

Action 4: Listen to your own voice first. Everybody has an opinion. The one that counts the most in your life, though, is your own. Rather than constantly soliciting the advice of others before acting, see what rings most true to you as the starting point. Ever seen those bracelets with the abbreviation WWJD (What Would Jesus Do?) that people wear to remind themselves to live to a higher standard? When you're assessing a situation, consider a tweak on that concept and ask yourself WDIT (What Do I Think?) first—not what your parents, boss, spouse, friend group, or your followers on social would chime in on. This is about you.

Start by learning to recognize your own voice. It's usually your first thought or reaction before getting drowned out by others. Sometimes it comes in as an overall concept, phrase, or emotion—like "This is bad," "This feels wrong" or "Yay, this is wonderful." Focus on that thought, and make it as solid as possible. Explore why you feel that way, and commit to acting on it instead of seeking permission or validation from other people. Consider what happened as a result of listening to yourself. Did you have a better outcome or avoid a negative situation? Give yourself credit, which will reinforce the importance and practice of honoring your own voice first.

Action 5: Identify which circumstances help you thrive. Authenticity grows when you know yourself and are honest about what you need—like having food, shelter, and healthy relationships as a sustaining baseline. Pinpoint what you need to thrive by filling in the following categories.

I'm at my best when _____
[describe your physical/mental/emotional state].

In order to be my best, I require _____
[write down what it takes to get or keep you in that positive place].

Things that can be barriers or challenges to thriving include _____ *[list all factors]*.

I handle those challenges by _____
[note your solutions].

Here's an example to make this process more concrete. Let's say that you're at your best when you get enough rest and natural sunlight. You need to have a good night's sleep, take breaks and days off, and spend as much time outdoors as possible. However, things that can be barriers include staying up too late watching TV each night and skimping on shut-eye, or a recurring case of seasonal affective disorder (SAD), a type of depression that most often starts in the fall and continues throughout the winter, triggered by shorter days and being cooped up inside. You handle those challenges by planning a consistent bedtime routine and curbing TV watching beforehand; or dealing with your SAD by increasing your exposure to daylight or light therapy, checking out psychotherapy and/or medications, and including daily activities that bring you more peace.

Action 6: Take an accurate self-inventory. Sometimes your self-view is trapped in the past, and you're trying to solve old problems that may have been resolved ten or fifteen years ago. Think about how your current friends, coworkers, and others would describe you today. Compare that to your current perceptions of who you are, whether that has to do with your career, relationships, state of health and wellness, financial well-being, or any other area of your life.

Exercise: Inward Trust Fall

If you've ever been to a corporate retreat or seen a movie parody about one, you may be familiar with the concept of a "trust fall"—when people surrounded by their peers close their eyes and lean backward, trusting that they'll be caught by those around them before hitting the ground. It was designed to be an exercise to build camaraderie and trust with the people one works with, kind of like when people dive into a mosh pit at a concert with the belief that the crowd will pass them around before being laid back gently on the ground.

But rather than relying on others, an inward trust fall is about releasing your past beliefs and obstacles. No closing of eyes or falling is necessary. The goal is to build trust with yourself by leaning inside. You learn that you can count on yourself to create a safe internal space of exploration that promotes your well-being. Start by choosing something small that you can achieve in order to build more confidence, and then you can gradually reach for more as your self-trust grows. Some steps that you can take include the following:

1. Find a quiet space where you can think clearly without any interruptions.

2. Get grounded. I mean this literally as well as figuratively. Sit in a comfortable chair that supports your body; and make sure that your feet are firmly planted on the floor, earth, or surface beneath you. Take a few deep breaths and clear your mind.

3. Set an intention. Make it clear, specific, and attainable. Rather than stating that you want to be in the best shape of your life or lose an unsustainable number of pounds overnight, go more granular here with statements such as: "I intend to exercise four to five days a week," or "I will eat at least three servings of fruits and vegetables each day."

4. Plan your implementation. Looking at the span of the week ahead, decide exactly how you'll bring that intention to life. Let's go with the example of incorporating four to five days' worth of exercise over the next seven days. Look at your calendar and determine when you plan to exercise, the duration, and the type of movement. Will you start with a fifteen-minute walk at lunch and then slowly increase it to thirty minutes? Or will you sign up for early-morning spin classes at a gym and lay your workout attire and gear out the night before to ensure that you get out the door? Be realistic, and don't choose something so far out of your current abilities that it's unachievable. Anticipate all of the details and potential obstacles in advance. If you'd like extra support, use the vision-board exercise (in chapter 3), seeing yourself achieving this intention.

5. Execute your goal. Do what you say you're going to do. Remember, it doesn't need to be perfect. Aim for consistency as you build this new behavior or practice.

6. Notice how you feel. You set a goal and achieved it. How does that make you feel? Proud? Scared? A combination of both? What was the outcome? How does this impact your confidence? From this place, what is possible next?

7. Acknowledge this personal win. Pat yourself on the back; then repeat this exercise as you apply it to other areas of your life.

CHAPTER 6
Give Yourself Permission

As a kid, you needed a couple of things to succeed in school. Along with the right textbooks and good study habits was the all-important permission slip signed by a parent or guardian. That official authorization was your golden ticket to attend school trips, sporting events, and participate in extracurricular activities. Without it, you were limited or lost. These days, as a grown-up, you don't often have to obtain that kind of consent to do your own thing. But when it comes to getting unstuck, actively giving yourself permission to change is crucial. The act of doing so ensures that all parts of you are aligned with your new behaviors and beliefs. This chapter teaches you how to give yourself permission—and use the confidence and trust you built in the previous chapter to fend off the negative inner voice that may stand in the way of change.

What It Means to Give Yourself Permission

At this point, you may be thinking that it's unnecessary to give yourself permission to change or choose a new direction. After all, reading this book means that you have more than a passing desire to get unstuck. However, many of us have formed a pattern of behaviors and beliefs over the years that could be deeply entrenched. These behaviors and beliefs—the type that you identified in yourself in chapter 1—are often the same things holding you back. It's not as easy as simply snapping your fingers, saying, "I will no longer be a Debbie Downer," and—presto—everything is better.

Self-doubt can creep in to sabotage you, which is why the previous chapter was all about building your self-confidence and self-trust. Now it's time to harness that confidence to give yourself permission to make the shift that will propel you forward. Instead of asking someone else if it's okay to proceed, authorizing your own course of action means that you trust yourself to make the right decisions. You're taking *ownership* of the process. It cements your belief in yourself, which increases your self-assurance and effectiveness.

When it comes down to it, granting yourself permission is about empowerment. It demonstrates your complete commitment to getting unstuck. It's akin to taking a pledge, or an oath of sorts, to consciously move forward in a positive manner and take charge. You're jumping into the driver's seat, and you're confident in your ability to plan ahead and make decisions that will help you reach your destination. Empowering yourself in this manner can create greater fulfillment and self-esteem. In fact, a 2005 study out of Hong Kong found a link between empowerment and life satisfaction.[1] Over a six-month period, researchers randomly sampled members of one hundred self-help groups that supported individuals who were chronically ill, were facing a physical or mental disability, were dealing with mental illness, or were part of other vulnerable populations. Participants completed a structured questionnaire on the same day their groups met. Researchers found that individuals who embraced personal empowerment experienced greater life satisfaction.[2]

There's a lot at risk when you don't green-light this process. Not putting your stake in the ground can limit your agency. Because so many of us are used to receiving permission from others throughout our lives—parents, teachers, bosses, and more—people who want to change can still become trapped in a pattern of waiting for others to approve their actions. And although a support system will help you achieve your goals (see chapter 10), other people cannot *lead* your transformation. Only you can.

Making the deliberate choice to grant yourself permission starts with your mind, but it often conjures up conflicting emotional reactions. There may be a thrill of excitement about what is possible, as well as fear about doing something different. Don't be surprised if you oscillate back and forth between relief and anxiousness. Just remember that when you do give yourself permission to get unstuck, it will ultimately open up tremendous opportunities and expansion in all parts of your life. Therapist and bestselling author Nedra Tawwab agrees. "When you give yourself permission, you are able to enjoy the fruits of your labor," she said in an interview for *Shine*. "Permission says that you are open to the possibility of positive things happening. Without permission, there is no growth."[3]

In order to deal with conflicting feelings, you'll probably need to let go of circumstances that no longer work for you. Tightly grasping something you've outgrown will only hold you back and potentially add to your emotional angst. Take, for example, a woman I'll call Jill, who was somewhat shy in college. She relied on her outgoing friend Kelsey to organize their social outings. After graduation, Kelsey continued to relish her self-appointed role as social director by scheduling bar crawls and tailgating parties. Jill kept attending gatherings over the next few years because she didn't want to disappoint Kelsey, but she felt disconnected from the activities. She was thriving professionally as an accountant and was also in a serious relationship, but she was exhausted by the continual social merry-go-round. Her idea of a good time was one-on-one dinners with friends or bingeing movies with her partner on their couch. Finally, she gave herself permission to stop accepting every invitation from Kelsey. And to her surprise, there was no drama. Kelsey just wanted Jill to feel included and was thrilled to see her friend happy and settled.

Once Jill got over doing what she felt she had to do versus what her heart truly wanted—and stopped the defeatist self-talk about being a loser for not wanting a packed social calendar—her sense of empowerment and confidence soared.

Speaking of negative self-talk, have you ever seen the over-the-top trash talk of professional athletes or the dramatic side-eye moments when reality-show stars put each other down? Your harsh inner voice—you know, that little soundtrack in your mind that whispers trash about you to you—can put those shenanigans to shame. It thrives by constantly trafficking in doubt, blame, regret, and humiliation and thinking that the worst is always about to happen.

Sure enough, that internal naysayer has a name. In the professional coaching community, we refer to it as the "inner saboteur" or "inner critic." In her book *Thrive*, Arianna Huffington calls it her "obnoxious roommate." Whatever moniker you use, those inner voices are true frenemies, similar to people who might like you until you're happier or more successful than they are. They pretend to be on your side, spewing bad advice under the guise of keeping you safe, but in reality, they hold you back. It's like the bully in third grade who took your lunch money in lieu of "beating you up," or the sorority sister who commends you for relying on your personality instead of your looks. The inner critic can be a real jerk.

Negative self-talk can also be one of the biggest challenges in giving yourself permission to get unstuck. It can be difficult to diminish that inner voice once it has been in residency for so long. If you've spent years or decades repeating the same negative mantra to yourself, that message may have gotten deeply entrenched. As you'll soon see, the inner saboteur doesn't like change—especially when it could mean being sidelined or permanently silenced.

Shirzad Chamine, a Stanford University lecturer and C-suite adviser, wrote a breakthrough book called *Positive Intelligence* about these mental foes. The book's premise is that only 20 percent of individuals and teams achieve their true potential because we spend a large amount of time sabotaging ourselves. That's astounding, right?

These insidious critics create stress and hurt your confidence. Research has shown that negative self-talk can contribute to anxiety[4] and depression.[5] As described in a February 2020 article on Verywell Mind titled "Toxic Effects of Negative Self-Talk," consequences include limited thinking, perfectionism, increased risk of depression, and relationship challenges.[6] Your potential to thrive and succeed is diminished, as critical thoughts about the prospect of failure or embarrassment keep you from reaching higher. Inner saboteurs are also an equal-opportunity culprit. I don't care if you're the CEO of a Fortune 100 company or a part-time cashier—we've all had these critical thoughts chime in at some point.

The good news is that with awareness, you can do something about it. Part of granting yourself permission means making a conscious decision to no longer listen to your inner saboteur. Giving yourself permission to transform weakens that inner critic because it inherently means that you're choosing to rely on what Chamine calls "your inner sage," or internal fountain of wisdom. The work you've completed in the previous chapters to understand your purpose and build self-confidence are wells to draw from when you need fortification against your inner saboteur.

Confronting your inner saboteur can be more challenging when you've relied on negative reinforcement for an extended period of time. Perhaps a coach shouting that your high school field hockey team sucked caused you to push harder and win a big game, or you had a breakthrough at work when you were determined to prove that a supervisor's criticisms were wrong. However, adopting negative self-talk as a motivational strategy can hurt you in the long term.

Let's delve more deeply into the field of sports as an example. In a 2017 article called "Self-Talk and Sports Performance" published by Oxford University Press, authors Judy L. Van Raalte and Andrew Vincent of Springfield College in Massachusetts found that both instructional and motivational self-talk have been shown to enhance performance on the playing field. While negative self-talk increases motivation and performance in some circumstances, it is generally detrimental to athletic performance. The same is true in your career and personal life.[7]

Of course, the inner critic rarely goes away quietly. When you start to make real, deep-down change—as you're about to do—it tends to get louder. Don't be surprised if the inner saboteur becomes hyperactive as you prepare to get unstuck. Hanging on by its claws, it can throw out numerous roadblocks in the form of doubting, self-critical thoughts. Recognizing the voice of the inner critic when it starts chiming in can help you fend it off quickly. That is one of the strategies used by leadership coach Laurie Arron, who is also the chief of staff at a major telecommunications corporation. It doesn't matter how many accolades Arron racks up, though. Her inner saboteur still tries to wriggle in with self-defeating thoughts. "The inner saboteur has a powerful voice, and it's in all of us fighting for a seat at the table when we're feeling vulnerable," noted Arron during our conversation. "I've learned that instead of trying to make the saboteur go away permanently, the most effective route is to not empower it, because I don't want my saboteur to get in the way of achieving the things I want in life."

Arron has given herself permission to take away her inner saboteur's power. She started by becoming aware of how it sounded in order to recognize the critic at work. Then she developed strategies to defuse its impact, such as deliberately pausing to examine the inner critic's thoughts and dismiss them as untrue. "The thought doesn't define us; it is just a thought," she explained. "Noticing that voice can make it go away pretty fast."

You'll have to learn what your inner critic sounds like to *you*. Pay attention to its voice and what circumstances trigger that negative chatter. Being able to recognize its tone immediately and dismiss it takes practice, but eventually that can become second nature. In the Take Action section, you'll learn specific tips for dealing with and diminishing your inner saboteur.

Case Study: Moe Mitchell

Giving himself permission to take a different path changed the trajectory of Moe Mitchell's life. He decided to green-light a transformation toward being more authentic and more open to new possibilities. You may have heard Moe on the radio or a podcast or seen one of his videos online. He's the cohost of the nationally syndicated radio program *The Bert Show*, and a successful comedian. But his road in life has not been easy.

Growing up, like many men in his generation, Moe was taught to keep his feelings in, put his head down, and not show any vulnerability. He dreamed about being a songwriter, so he moved back to New York in his early twenties to try to make things happen after college. He worked every job he could: fast food, retail, marketing; and he was even a paralegal for a while. But he struggled financially, trying to live on his own in such an expensive city. At one point, Moe became temporarily homeless, living out of his car for a week because he was too ashamed to ask his grandmother, who lived nearby, for help.

"That was my true rock bottom," he said. "It's a dark place to be, because you can't really see too far outside of it and believe it is the worst things are ever going to be. But you can come out of that as a brand-new person. All I had was my faith and belief in myself. I deliberately let go of my pride and told the universe I was open to what's next. Then doors began to open, slowly but surely."

Moe got a job working at a radio station as a mail carrier, having no clue that, three years later, he would become a radio personality himself. He tried comedy on the side, turning open-mic nights into viral videos. He kept trying to come up with a viral-video concept based on what he thought others wanted to see, but nothing was working. Then he stopped trying so hard and gave himself permission to just be. His grandmother had instilled a love for astrology in him, and one day while sitting with friends, Mitchell cracked everyone up by making fun of their astrological signs. He decided to make a video poking fun at Scorpios, and it broke a hundred thousand views. The rest of his hilarious zodiac-sign videos were even bigger hits online.

"Everything changed the moment I stopped trying to do what I thought people wanted me to do and simply did what was already in my heart," said Moe. "It was there the entire time. All I had to do was be myself."

That success led to Moe being recruited to join the cast of *The Bert Show*. He moved a thousand miles away from home, joining a broadcast format that required openness and vulnerability in front of an audience of millions. Moe has authentically shared personal challenges on the air that resonate deeply with his listeners, like being physically abused as a child by his father, the systemic racism he has faced being Black, and personal setbacks with relationships—all of which has had a ripple effect in encouraging others to give themselves permission to be more authentic.

"Moving to Atlanta with no family and no friends, to do a job I've never done in an industry I didn't know, was one of the scariest things I'd ever had to do," Moe said. "I was afraid, and that's exactly why I did it. Giving myself permission to be the real me turned out to be one of the best decisions I've ever made in my life."

Take Action

Giving yourself permission to get unstuck is an important part of this process. Arming yourself with the following tactics will allow you to become more comfortable with granting yourself permission, weakening the inner critic, and surging forward to effect positive change:

Action 1: Practice giving yourself permission. If you've been doing and thinking things a certain way for a while, it's often more effective to practice giving yourself permission to change in small ways. Maybe you've gotten in the habit of having lunch with your significant other's family every Sunday, come rain or come shine. It's expected, and you resent it. You'd like to occasionally travel out of town or be more spontaneous on Sundays. One time you turned down an opportunity to catch up with an overseas friend you hadn't seen in years who happened to be in town. When you started to question it, your inner critic popped in with the thoughts, *The in-laws won't like me anymore if I make waves*, and *I'll let my partner down if I do something for myself.* You accused yourself of being thoughtless or selfish. As a result, you've never brought up the possibility of skipping a Sunday to your partner.

To complete this action, you could grant yourself permission to discuss the Sunday lunch with your partner and redesign your participation terms. You allow yourself to say that, sometimes, you need to do something else on Sundays instead. The next time you need time for yourself, give yourself permission to bow out of lunch. Perhaps no one will mind at all. Or perhaps people will question you. In that case, protect your decision and do not waver from it. Remind yourself that you've attended hundreds of Sunday lunches, and that it's not selfish to take an occasional afternoon for yourself. Life changes, and so do our own needs.

Action 2: Acknowledge your inner voice. Unfortunately, trying to ignore negative self-talk can be ineffective. Rather than stick your fingers in your ears and chant "I can't hear you," pause and listen intently to what your inner saboteur has to say. Often those comments originally stemmed from a desire to protect yourself from danger—real or imagined—and along the way, they got twisted into a negativity fest. One way to acknowledge your inner voice is by journaling, which you'll learn more about in chapter 12. After noting what the inner saboteur is trying to express, thank that voice for any original positive intent or benefit that might have been gained from its protection in the past. Then articulate how you've outgrown those beliefs and why it's time to behave differently now.

You can also talk this through out loud, if the spoken word is easier that writing things down. The process is the same. Acknowledge your inner saboteur's initial positive intent, if that was the case, and then reaffirm that it is no longer needed. Ideally this is done when you're alone, but you can always stick earbuds in and pretend the conversation is taking place with another person.

Action 3: Name your inner saboteur. When you think of the inner critic as a mysterious, lurking force, the critic gets more power. To demystify the critic, give it a name. I named mine Resting Bitch Face, or RBF for short. You've probably heard this term before, as it applies to the judgmental or stern expression on people's faces even when their facial muscles are neutral. These individuals might be delightful when you get to know them, but the lack of a friendly smile causes you to pause and assume the worst. For me, it's the perfect term to remind myself that my inner critic is not always what it seems. So choose a name that disarms your *own* inner critic.

Action 4: Shift the conversation. We all have bad days sometimes. That's when the inner saboteur thinks it can climb back in and reestablish residency after you've said goodbye. The key is to recognize when its whispers start, and shut them down immediately. Listen to your words, and instead of focusing on "I should" or "I need to," regain perspective by pivoting to "I can" or "I choose to." Practice positive affirmations to quiet the inner saboteur, because those statements of gratitude ring truer than critical inner thoughts. It can also be effective to shift the inner criticism to praise based on what you like about yourself. For example, you could change "I'm never going to wear that dress size again" to "Look at that kick-ass muscle tone in my arms—who cares about a number on a label!" Repeat those positive statements like a mantra until they banish the negative chatter.

Action 5: Engage in "thought-stopping" exercises. I've come across a couple of exercises to stop negative self-talk when you catch it in action. If you're actively trying to break this habit, consider wearing a rubber band around your wrist, and snap it each time you have a self-deprecating thought. Admittedly, this isn't a great fashion choice, but the physical sensation of catching and cutting off the criticism can help change your habits. Maybe you say "Stop!" out loud to yourself until it passes. I've seen people play the first few bars of a song on their digital devices to drown it out. A few old-school tunes to consider for their immediate catchiness: "Hey Mickey" by Toni Basil, "Hey Ya!" by Outkast, and "Bootylicious" by Destiny's Child. It's hard to sustain negative self-talk when you're being encouraged to "shake it like a Polaroid picture," right?

Action 6: Make it less personal. In a June 2017 *New York Times* article titled "The Benefits of Talking to Yourself," University of Michigan psychology professor Ethan Kross, PhD, noted that how you refer to yourself in self-talk can make a difference. In studying the impact of internal self-talk, Kross's team found that when subjects talked about themselves in the second or third person (for example, "You can do this" or "Shira can do this" instead of "I can do this"), they felt less anxiety while performing, and peers also rated their performances better. Consider listing the reasons why "you" rather than "I" are going to soar instead of suck at a particular task. Write them down, and then say it out loud, replacing negative self-talk with a more positive version. It works.

Action 7: Recognize progress. Take an assessment to monitor improvements in your inner saboteur over time. When I first completed Chamine's online Saboteur Assessment in March 2016 (which you can find at PositiveIntelligence.com), my top saboteur was identified as something called the Pleaser. It "indirectly tries to gain acceptance and affection by helping, pleasing, rescuing, or flattering others" and "loses sight of own needs and becomes resentful as a result."[8] Bingo—that certainly rang true. On a scale of 1 to 10, I scored a 9, which is quite high—but also beneficial because I could clearly see this dominant inner saboteur at work. It didn't mean that I was less in some way, but rather, more honest about who I was and the challenges I needed to overcome to enjoy a more fulfilling life. After engaging in many of these actions over a sustained period of time, it diminished the power of my inner critic. I took the assessment again in 2020, and my Pleaser saboteur level had dropped to a 5. Seeing that numerical progress affirmed that I was on the right track, and I continue to savor that win. Rather than waiting years between assessments, you may want to check in every six months after intentionally working to diminish dominant saboteur behavior.

Exercise: Create Your Own Permission Slip

We've talked a lot about granting yourself permission to change, make different choices, and take other actions in order to get unstuck. Now it's time to create your own permission slip to fully activate the power of this step. Use the template below by filling in the blanks with your details and desired intentions.

> I, [your name], am granting myself official permission to [your intended change].
>
> I will no longer be [type of stuck from chapter 2] by [characteristic behavior]. This means that I will no longer engage in: [three to five actions or behaviors that epitomize your stuck].
>
> What I claim instead is [specific goal]. I am bringing that to life by [actions you plan to take].
>
> Your signature: _____
>
> Activation date (day, month, year): _____

Sample Permission Slip

Here's how a completed permission slip could look, using the above template:

> I, Jennifer Smith, am granting myself official permission to get unstuck and build more satisfying romantic connections.
>
> I will no longer be a Debbie Downer by expecting each potential romantic partner to let me down in some way. That means I will no longer engage in (1) expecting the worst to constantly happen, (2) pushing away people I like after a couple of dates to avoid getting hurt, and (3) obsessively searching a prospective partner's social feeds for clues about character flaws.
>
> Instead, what I claim is a happy, long-term romantic relationship. I am bringing that to life by (1) assuming that things will work out when I'm interested in someone, (2) practicing more

open communication, (3) staying in the moment during dates and really enjoying the process of getting to know someone who interests me, and (4) being willing to be the first one to express how I feel and request dating exclusivity, if that is what I desire.

Jennifer Smith
Activation date: July 18, 2022

This template works for any of the types of stuck outlined in chapter 2. Just fill in the details related to your specific goals and circumstances. (You can download this permission slip at ShiraMiller.com if you'd like to access it in that format.)

Once completed, don't let this permission slip languish in a forgotten spot. Revisit it regularly, whether once a week or twice a year or some other time frame, to reinforce your intentions. Save it as a PDF and print it. Insert it in a picture frame or a laminated sheet to protect the piece if you prefer having something that can be touched. Or, you could save it to a smart device for easy access.

Part Three

Taking Action

CHAPTER 7

Become Resilient

AT THIS POINT, you've done your homework by taking a strategic pause, identifying your purpose, building self-trust, and giving yourself permission to change. Talk about being an A student! Now it's time to utilize that preparation to start taking action. In this chapter, you'll learn how to increase your resilience, which is the ability to bounce back from adversity, obstacles, and challenges—you know, the very things that could have triggered your stuckness.

It's possible that you made a mistake or that someone else has wronged you. Or you do everything "right," but the universe has thrown you a curveball that seems unfair. You may have experienced severe loss, trauma, or feelings of failure. Within the context of this step, being resilient means facing these challenges head-on: taking ownership when needed and letting go when it's not, trusting that you can and will figure things out, becoming more flexible in order to handle whatever lies ahead in your personal and professional life, and learning how to forgive yourself and others so you can remove the emotional burden of unforgiveness and become more open to receiving more goodness moving forward.

Increasing your resilience will allow you to better handle future challenges and avoid getting stuck when the chips are down, which makes this kind of adaptability crucial as you break free from your stuck place. It also prepares you to fully embrace the other action steps in this section, such as choosing positivity and pivoting with purpose.

What It Means to Become Resilient

Yes, flexibility is an important part of becoming resilient. You need to be able to shift your behavior and perspective in order to adapt to new circumstances and overcome misfortunes. But resilience also comprises your attitude and your belief in yourself. It's about trusting your competence and staying the course toward fulfilling your purpose.

That's what researchers Kathryn Connor and Jonathan Davidson determined after developing the Connor-Davidson Resilience scale (CD-RISC)[1] to assess resilience in individuals. Their research found that resilient people have certain characteristics, such as commitment and self-efficacy (which you learned about in chapter 5); seeking support and close relationships (which is covered in chapter 10); viewing change as a challenge or opportunity; and adaptability, patience, and optimism.[2]

In almost every definition of resilience I've seen, a component of overcoming hardship is present. Researcher and psychology professor Suniya S. Luthar, PhD, has said that resilience is positive adaptation despite adversity, noting that both dimensions—being able to respond constructively to the circumstance and having to deal with a significant level of adversity—are present.[3] In other words, people who can harness their inner strength—which you developed in the last chapter—are better equipped to overcome misfortune.

How individuals respond to adversity varies from person to person. Some people who don't get into their dream graduate programs may resolve to work harder and get in the following year, while others might give up and settle on jobs that make them miserable. Developmental psychologist Emmy Werner, PhD, described resilience as being displayed in three ways: (1) having good developmental outcomes despite high-risk status, (2) sustained competence under stress, and (3) recovery from trauma.[4]

Let's take a look at each. Having good outcomes despite being high-risk describes a nine-year-old boy whom developmental psychologist Norman Garmezy, PhD, worked with. The boy was being raised by a single parent, an alcoholic mom. The child wasn't being cared for and didn't have food at home; he would make himself a sandwich out of two pieces of bread to eat during lunch with other kids to avoid eliciting sympathy. Despite his difficult circumstances, though, he excelled in school. Sustained competence under stress brings to mind TV news anchor Katie Couric, who became one of the highest-paid broadcast personalities in 1998, during the same time her husband died after a six-month battle with colon cancer, leaving her to raise two young daughters.

As for recovery from trauma, which is an emotional response to a terrible event, I think of Congresswoman Lucy McBath. When her seventeen-year-old son was killed in an act of senseless violence, the two-time breast-cancer survivor left her thirty-year career as a flight attendant to become a national advocate for gun control and then run for office. Her recovery and healing process involved trying to make a positive difference by being of service to others.

In each circumstance, these individuals dealt with significant adversity that could have left them deeply, permanently stuck. But it didn't, because they each displayed a level of resilience that allowed them to overcome difficult circumstances and ultimately thrive.

You may or may not be facing those types of traumatic situations, and you may or may not have that level of resilience. Martin E. P. Seligman, PhD, one of the originators of the field of positive psychology and the director of the Penn Positive Psychology Center, said that a key difference between those who give up and those who don't is optimism: they have "a habit of interpreting setbacks as temporary, local, and changeable."[5] Optimists gravitate toward the positive and expect good outcomes. Seligman believes that you can cultivate resilience by learning how to think like an optimist, even if it's not your natural tendency. I've experienced that personally and believe that it's true for nearly anyone looking to adopt that mindset. Focusing on what's going well and the benefits gained from a challenging experience or situation can boost your optimism and ability to handle setbacks, as you'll see in the Take Action section—and so can practicing gratitude, which is covered in depth in chapter 8.

Seligman's concept of "learned optimism"[6] led him to create the Penn Resiliency Program, which educates people in how to improve their ability to handle adversity. The program does so by focusing on teaching participants skills like managing self-talk, learning optimism, cultivating gratitude, avoiding thinking traps, leading with values and strengths, and building better relationships with others.

These resiliency skills can be learned, but you don't have to take an immersive education course to become more resilient. Many of these concepts are covered throughout *Free and Clear*. Depending on your emotional and mental state, making a few shifts, such as choosing to focus on what is gained versus lost or how you've grown, can help. For example, when my public relations firm failed after the Great Recession in 2009, I could have felt broken for the rest of my career. And I did for a while. But with time and perspective, I realized that my experience allowed me to help others heal, and it became the basis of my 2019 TEDx talk called "5 Ways to Let Go of a Dream."

Seligman and his colleagues also created a program to teach resiliency to the one million–plus members of the US Army, where trauma is an everyday part of life. Seligman believes that resiliency in the army, as in the broader population, follows a normal distribution curve: at one end of the spectrum are people who cannot overcome their trauma and suffer in the long term from PTSD and depression; in the middle are most people, who may experience PTSD, depression, and anxiety in the short term before returning to where they were before the trauma; and then on the other end of the spectrum are those who experience the symptoms of trauma in the short term but then rebound to a better place than they were before the ordeal. Seligman calls this "post-traumatic growth" and believes that people can self-improve to get closer to this part of the curve.[7]

Two psychology professors at the University of North Carolina in Charlotte, Richard G. Tedeschi, Ph.D., and Lawrence G. Calhoun, Ph.D., first introduced the concept of post-traumatic growth in the 1990s as the experience of positive transformation after trauma. In this sense, trauma was very broadly defined as anything from a death in the family to divorce, physical trauma, or a work-related loss. Bottom line, their research and resulting publications indicated that negative experiences can spur a deeper understanding of oneself and a greater appreciation for life, which aligns with Seligman's work.

Ludmila N. Praslova, PhD, the director of research for graduate organizational psychology at Vanguard University in Southern California, agrees. "The key idea is that some people may develop a greater personal strength, experience spiritual changes, and come to see new possibilities, themselves, and relationships in a different light," she said when we spoke. Praslova shared the experience of her grandmother, who lived right on the path of the Nazi "Drive to the East" during World War II. In pressing toward Moscow, "the Nazis would basically take entire villages, put them around columns, and use them as living shields, and my grandmother was in one with her five children. She always said that after surviving that and saving her children, she could do anything."

As noted earlier, believing in your competence is a component of resilience because it means that you trust yourself to make good decisions and perform well. According to the University of Victoria, "A competency is made up of the following three elements: skill, knowledge and attribute." A skill is something that you excel at, like knowing how to bake the perfect sourdough bread every time or being able to easily translate documents into a second language. Knowledge is about knowing your stuff, practices, and information, such as being the expert on cybersecurity at work or serving as the "go to" volunteer to solicit corporate donations for a nonprofit. Attributes are your personal characteristics, like your ability to use humor to defuse tense situations or how you can stay calm during chaotic times. Recognizing and trusting your competencies builds resilience because it strengthens your internal foundation (as you've worked on in the previous chapters), better equipping you to handle challenges and adapt as needed.

In addition to cultivating optimism and trusting your competence, practicing forgiveness can help you become more resilient. Forgiveness, as highlighted in chapter 2, is an intentional act to release negative feelings toward someone who has hurt you, which can include yourself. An unwillingness to consider forgiveness—of others or yourself—is one of the 7 Things That Gets You Stuck. When you release the negative energy spent on unforgiveness—resentment, judgment, bitterness, and more—it frees you to move forward and rebound more fully from the circumstance that caused you pain or harm.

Research has shown a direct link between forgiveness and resilience. A study reported in the *Indian Journal of Mental Health* in 2016 found that forgiveness increases resilience.[8] A 2005 University of Tennessee study conducted of nearly five hundred people over the age of fifty living in the southeastern United States demonstrated that, as forgiveness increases, resilience does, too.[9]

Forgiveness also makes you stronger and better able to withstand challenges. As forgiveness researcher Everett Worthington, PhD, Commonwealth Professor Emeritus of Virginia Commonwealth University, explained, "Forgiveness is often difficult, and when we are tested and rise to the challenge, it strengthens us. That strengthening helps us bounce back in the wake of disasters and traumas. Forgiveness can help us become more resilient."[10]

Forgiving a trespass isn't just about the parties who committed harm; it is truly something that you engage in for yourself. You're not diminishing or forgetting the transgression that took place in any way by practicing forgiveness. Rather, I consider it a coping strategy that boosts your resilience by allowing you to let go of what may be keeping you stuck in place. Like optimism, forgiveness can be learned. (An exercise at the end of this chapter teaches you how to build your forgiveness muscles.)

Moving forward in forgiveness also benefits your well-being. As

Mason Turner, MD, Kaiser Permanente Northern California's director of outpatient mental health and addiction medicine, noted, forgiveness is a powerful act that can have lasting health benefits. He said that "the process of forgiveness for a serious offense can be long and difficult, but research shows forgiveness can lower your stress levels; boost your immune system; and help you to be a better friend, family member, and colleague."[11]

As mentioned earlier, sometimes the hardest person to forgive is yourself. That can be true whether you've done something harmful or illegal that requires a level of atonement, or if you haven't done anything wrong at all but are bringing yourself down with self-imposed guilt or contempt. Remember Richard Bistrong from chapter 2, who went to prison for corruption charges? He took full responsibility for his missteps and then dedicated his life to making amends. For Bistrong, self-forgiveness is about constantly taking accountability and actively sharing his story to reach others who could face similar circumstances. "Getting sentenced to prison helped me with forgiveness because I felt like there was finality to it," he noted. "I harmed my family, society, and several parties. Paying the ultimate price through the loss of liberty gave me some closure. There are two parts to forgiveness—the kind where you apologize to family and others, and then there is knitting amends. Sharing my story keeps what happened alive for me in a way that I won't forget."

After being released, Bistrong realized that no one was talking about foreign bribery from the commercial perspective. He wrote about his experiences, being up front that breaking the law was no one's fault but his own. Compliance and ethics symposiums started inviting Bistrong to speak. When his passport was returned post-probation, he began traveling to the parts of the world where corrupt practices are most prevalent. He built a successful practice helping organizations identify conflicting internal messages about acceptable behaviors and ethics, and he provides field training to prevent bribery.

Bistrong compares forgiveness to cycling uphill. "Forgiving yourself should not be easy," he added. "You must be transparent and embrace what you did. It should be a struggle filled with humility. Avoid minimizing what happened and its consequences. You don't ever get to the point of not talking about it anymore."

In the case of Bistrong, a transgression was committed that he sought to atone for. But let's say that you failed at something—a business venture that went sideways or an investment opportunity that flopped spectacularly. No one was harmed in that process, except yourself. Yet some people perceive failure as a death sentence of sorts, where their self-esteem and self-efficacy are permanently damaged. That's because our culture often stigmatizes failure as something to be avoided at any cost. In some cases, it can feel like a trauma from which you need to recover. That's when you need to leverage numerous characteristics of resilience—optimism, belief in your own competency, adaptability, and a willingness to forgive—in order to spring back from those circumstances. You can start by reframing the term *failure* to mean that you're taking chances and trying something different in pursuit of a goal. It creates an opportunity to learn, grow, and achieve even more over time.

Giving yourself context can help. Some of the most successful people in the world experienced and came back from failure. Oprah Winfrey, Steve Jobs, and Walt Disney were all fired from jobs along the way before achieving their greatest successes. It took Thomas Edison more than two thousand tries before he created the light bulb. It took five years and 5,126 failed prototypes for James Dyson to develop the world's first bagless vacuum cleaner. Iconic director Steven Spielberg was rejected both times he applied to film school at the University of Southern California.

Albert Einstein once said, "Success is failure in progress." That poster child for brilliance certainly knew a lot about the topic. Einstein didn't start talking until age four, was expelled from school, and was refused admittance to Zurich Polytechnic School, his top pick. Yet he still ended up winning the Nobel Prize for Physics in 1921.

What matters is that in facing failure, you keep on going despite the emotional turmoil. Lick your wounds, try to find the lesson, and move on. Think about luminaries in your desired path who failed and then came back much better or bigger than before. Resilience was essential in their positive outcomes, and it will be for you as well. Think about how you can reframe failure as just another step in having a fulfilling, purpose-filled life.

Case Study: Alyson Gondek

The journey to self-forgiveness was challenging for Alyson Gondek. When her elderly mother was diagnosed with Alzheimer's, she took on the entire burden of caring for her mom's finances and well-being. In 2017, Alyson was shocked to learn that her mother's financial adviser had mishandled her funds.

Along with her brother and sister, Alyson conducted a financial investigation in the hopes of recouping some of the money that was taken fraudulently. After an incredibly draining sixteen-month process, they settled through mediation. They recovered some of the money, but the majority of it went to attorney fees. Then Alyson's sister double-crossed them, threatening to sue her siblings for financial mismanagement if she didn't receive a large portion of the remaining settlement. It left their mother with almost nothing.

Right after the onset of the COVID-19 pandemic, Alyson had to pack up and relocate her mother to a more cost-effective memory-care center. The difficult, double betrayal left Alyson racked with guilt and frustration, especially as her mother's health continued to decline. "I felt responsible for what happened to her, that I should have somehow caught this financial adviser and known my sister would pull the rug out from under us," explained Alyson. "I would just literally be tearing up every single day, unable to forgive myself for this happening to my mom."

Alyson felt embarrassed and humiliated despite the fact that none of the situation was her fault. She prayed frequently, visited her mother often, and received spiritual guidance from the chaplains at the long-term-care facility. Alyson found it cathartic to write, penning letters with health updates to her mother's friends. Her husband and adult daughters were incredibly supportive, reinforcing the fact that Alyson was not to blame and that it could have happened to anyone.

"One of my girls told me that you can't just live like this forever. You don't want to be this upset for the rest of your life" said Alyson, who felt that this conversation was a turning point. "I saw that by being miserable and not forgiving myself, I was being selfish and hurting everyone around me. And since I did nothing wrong, then I had to move on."

These conversations, as well as turning to her faith, helped Alyson become more resilient. She started to move past the self-inflicted shame. When her mother passed in April 2020, Alyson completely released the negative feelings and embraced forgiveness.

"I finally decided that I could forgive myself, and that the best thing was to put it all behind me and move forward in a positive light," she noted. "A lot of it is trusting in divine intervention and focusing on internal, positive messaging, making sure that you feel confident knowing that you did nothing wrong. My wish for others dealing with similar situations is to forgive and move on at the pace you need. Life is too short to live in guilt."

Take Action

The process of becoming more resilient starts with taking a baseline measurement. You may need to recognize your self-efficacy and competencies, learn how to become more optimistic, and practice forgiveness in order to shift your perspective and become more flexible overall.

Action 1: Rate your resilience. Take a baseline measurement to determine your current level of resilience. (If you'd like to do this yourself, MindTools.com offers a quick, free assessment online that gives you a score with a general interpretation of what it means.) You can also work with a therapist or coach to take one of the popular resilience-assessment tools like the Connor-Davidson Resilience Scale mentioned earlier, the Resilience Scale for Adults, the Brief Resilience Scale, Predictive 6-Factor Resilience Scale, and several others. Whatever you choose, determine your baseline level now so that you can measure it again after working to strengthen your resilience skills. When it feels like you've made a real shift—whether that's in eight weeks or eight months—take the same assessment again. Hopefully, you'll see measurable progress.

Action 2: Notice the good things. Anyone can become more optimistic with clear intentions and practice. One way to get started is to start noticing what's going right. Each day before going to sleep, record what went well in your world. Commit to finding at least three good things daily, but feel free to write down as many items as possible on a smart device or on paper—for example, a good checkup with your dentist; you were running late, but the bus waited for you; you found an unexpected $20 bill in a jacket pocket; your boss praised you at a company meeting—you get the idea. Do this every day for a month and see how things change. It may feel as if there's more positive in your life even if the same things were taking place all along and you're just noticing them for the first time. Being aware of the good things in your life will increase your optimism and bolster your resilience as a result.

Action 3: Build resilience resonance. Consider a time when you displayed strong resilience. Perhaps it involved healing after a painful breakup and then improving your relationship with yourself, or losing a job only to find an even better one a short time later. What helped you bounce back from that situation into improved circumstances? What would you like to acknowledge about yourself that made a difference?

Action 4: Allow space and grace. Sure, you might need time to heal from difficult circumstances, so be kind to yourself as you do so. When you're ready, engaging in forgiveness can help you bounce back from adversity. (The How to Practice Forgiveness exercise at the end of this chapter will guide you in that process.)

Action 5: Cultivate a diverse network. Opening your mind to new ideas and resources can help you learn, grow, and become more resilient personally and professionally. Being able to turn to a far-ranging network allows you to hear about opportunities and alternative sources of information that will help you become more adaptable. For example, you can search articles all day long online on a topic of interest, but being able to engage with someone else who has lived through that circumstance can enrich your knowledge base and create new possibilities.

As I publish this book, my largest network is via LinkedIn. Because much of my career has been spent in corporate communications and coaching, I'm connected with many marketing, public relations, and executive coaching professionals. But I'm always looking to hear from thought leaders across the globe, authors, innovators, educators, and more who have something interesting to say and share. Leveraging that network has helped me find fascinating people to interview for this book and broaden my perspective overall.

Action 6: Develop your cross-training skills. Being able to bounce back from career setbacks or return after a planned hiatus often involves accessing a broader range of skills and knowledge. You can take online courses in a myriad of areas to learn new capabilities. I know a former massage therapist who learned how to code medical data when the COVID-19 pandemic sidelined her business, allowing her to build a more lucrative career not dependent on physically interacting with others. This is also a great time to develop foundational skills that support your career development, like learning how to use the latest presentation software or studying another language.

Action 7: Practice "Yes, and." Have you gotten used to the "either/or" paradigm, where a situation can only have two outcomes? It might be time to get better at the concept of "Yes, and," which is used by executive coaches and improv instructors alike to teach people how to expand their thinking and become more resilient. Let's say you're a runner and only identify with that type of physical activity, but all those long runs you took when training for your last 10K race caused hip and knee pain to flare up from overuse. Your initial reaction might be that if you can't run, then you aren't exercising at all. However, you can choose to expand your personal definition to be "Yes, I'm a runner, and I'm also an athlete who enjoys a lot of different activities." With that mindset, you might get more into yoga, spin classes, weight training, or rowing to become stronger and more fit overall while allowing your running-related injuries to heal.

Exercise: How to Practice Forgiveness

Making a conscious decision to practice forgiveness can help release emotional turmoil and negative energy. Detailed below is a combination of thinking and action steps; this process can be applied to forgiving others or yourself. Remember, forgiveness is a choice. Go deep to actively decide if you want to pursue forgiveness for your own growth and healing. Tap into what lies at the core of your values and purpose (identified in chapter 4). With your true desire in mind, determine if forgiveness will serve you or not at this time. If the answer is yes, keep reading on. If you're not ready yet, come back when it feels right.

When forgiving others, answer the questions below to plan how you'd like to proceed:

- Who are you contemplating forgiving?
- What were their transgressions? Were they intentional?
- Why do you want to forgive them?
- How will forgiving those individuals benefit you?
- Will your act of forgiveness be done on your own, or will you tell them? Either way, what would you like to say to the transgressors?

When forgiving yourself, answer the questions below to plan how you'd like to proceed:

- What are you forgiving yourself for?
- Have you actually done something wrong?
- Were your harmful actions intentional?
- Why do you want to forgive yourself?
- What would you like to say to the earlier version of yourself who committed this transgression?
- How will engaging in forgiveness benefit you?

Take physical action. At the top of a sheet of paper, write the names of the people you're forgiving. Then record what you'd like to say to them. At the bottom of the sheet, write what you plan to release from yourself with this act of forgiveness. For example, it could be self-doubt, anger, sabotaging relationships, or listening to someone else's criticism instead of trusting your own instincts.

Destroy that document, ceremoniously releasing the echoes of adversity that have been stuck within. One option is to burn it within a safe, contained place (that is, not a location with flammable objects). My preference? Simply put that sheet through a shredder or tear it into tiny pieces. Either way, you'll accomplish the symbolic destruction of what was holding you back.

With this act of releasing what you couldn't forgive in the past, identify what you'd like to embrace in its place. Greater peace? A healthier lifestyle? Write about that, or choose an image that will reinforce it, like the vision board you created in chapter 3.

Now it's time to reflect. What did you learn from this experience? What did it teach you about your capacity for resilience and growth?

CHAPTER 8
Choose Positivity

Our world is changing more quickly than ever before: economic fluctuations, political divisiveness, health crises, climate change, rampant disinformation, and more can make people feel out of control. But no matter what happens, you have the ability to choose how to perceive and respond to those circumstances. When it comes to deciding between optimism and pessimism, learning how to choose the positive option is an important step on your journey to becoming unstuck. Ever heard the phrase "the power of positive thinking"? Well, as it turns out, positivity is pretty powerful.

In the previous chapter, you learned how to become more resilient and bounce back from setbacks. We talked about how optimism is a facet of resilience, but it goes beyond that. It's so important that it requires its own chapter! And however unlikely it may seem now, you *can* learn how to be more authentically positive. This chapter is all about how you can make small changes to develop and maintain a more positive outlook. As you'll see in the pages ahead, research has shown that genuine positive thinking—not the "toxic positivity" that is about fake reassurances that dismisses difficult emotions—helps generate your desired outcomes. You will cultivate optimism and, in doing so, move yourself closer to thriving in your desired future state.

What It Means to Choose Positivity

Choosing positivity, like giving yourself permission to change, is about empowerment. It allows you to change your mindset: life no longer is happening *to* you but rather you are an active participant, driving the bus down a much more fulfilling and joyous road. You may recall from the Debbie Downer section of chapter 2 that many of us have cognitive distortions that make us see things more negatively than the reality. Well, you can make an authentic shift, where you retrain your mind to look at situations, people, and relationships from a slightly different, more encouraging (and often more objective) perspective. This process is called *cognitive reframing*, which means actively seeking the positive, anticipating good outcomes, embracing hope and joy, and adopting a growth mindset. We're going to cover each of those concepts here. The truth is that we don't always have to plan for the worst. We can plan for the best. And you'll be amazed by what can happen when you do.

In the previous chapter, you learned how optimism can increase resilience. It can also help you focus on gratitude (which we'll cover in chapter 13), increase well-being, improve your relationships with yourself and others, and help you become more creative.

Let's start with well-being. According to research conducted by Lisa R. Yanek and her colleagues at Johns Hopkins University, patients with a family history of heart disease who also had a positive outlook were one-third less likely to have a heart attack or other cardiovascular event within five to twenty-five years than those with a more negative outlook.[1] Even positive people who didn't have a history of heart disease were 13 percent less likely to have a cardiovascular event than their pessimistic counterparts! Yanek noted that their team determined "positive" versus "negative" outlook using a survey tool that assesses a person's cheerfulness, energy level, anxiety level, and satisfaction with health and overall life.[2] Additional studies have shown that a positive outlook can improve life satisfaction and the outcomes of conditions ranging from cancer, heart disease, strokes, and more.[3] It's not exactly known why positivity can impact health and well-being so much, but researchers speculate that positive people are more protected from stress, which has been shown to cause inflammatory damage.

Next up: relationships. Choosing positivity strengthens your relationships with others and yourself. As reported in the June 2018 issue of *Time* magazine, biological anthropologist and Kinsey Institute senior fellow Helen Fisher found three essential neuro-chemical components in people who report high relationship satisfaction: practicing empathy, controlling one's feelings and stress, and maintaining positive views about one's partner. Fisher noted that the latter component is about reducing the amount of time you spend thinking about the negative aspects of your relationship.[4] Research has also shown that the way a couple shares and supports good news with each other, as well as being there during hard times, strengthens relationships.[5] In a daily diary study of sixty-seven cohabiting couples that served as the basis for that research, study authors found that they felt stronger ties to their partners when sharing a happy event with them.

Monique Russell, an executive communications coach specializing in emotional intelligence, has seen that choosing positivity improves your relationship with yourself as well as others. "In seeking the positive, you'll have a better quality of life, you'll feel fulfilled, you'll feel excited, you'll feel that joy, and then you can put those walls down—the walls around your heart that prevent you from actually connecting and having a deeper relationship with others," she told me during our conversation.

When we spoke, change management consultant and coach Samantha Fowlds also noted that seeking positive learnings and growth from challenging experiences can also make you more creative and smarter. "Negative thoughts tend to narrow your focus and vision as you get into the animal instinct of fight or flight," said Fowlds, referencing researcher Barbara Frederickson's broaden-and-build theory of positive emotions. "Whereas when you're positive, your thoughts are expansive. You tend to be more creative, curious, ask questions, and learn more things that ultimately make you braver, stronger, and more resilient."

So how can you help yourself receive the benefits of positive thinking, even if your personality is naturally negative? Through cognitive reframing. And one way to reframe your mindset is by actively seeking the positive—finding the upside or silver lining by considering the positive perspectives of something you'd typically describe as negative. When you do so, you can turn problematic circumstances into opportunities for growth and fulfillment. Nancy Taylor, the chief education officer of Taylor Educational Advocacy, has clients develop their positivity muscles by placing themselves in multiple perspectives. She starts by applying that practice to herself. "As an example, rainy days get me down, and I feel the gray deeply and uncomfortably. When I start thinking that I don't like rainy days, I stop and say to myself that gray days are necessary for us to have plants that grow and water to drink," Taylor explained to me during our interview. "In this way, I reframe a negative into a positive for myself. I can mitigate the effects of the negative by finding a positive outcome or experience from it. Cognitive reframing can be done for most of the negative feelings and thoughts we have."

Another way to reframe your thinking is to plan for positive outcomes, though this may seem unnatural. Many cultural icons—from Stephen King to Maya Angelou—have said something to the effect of "Hope for the best but prepare for the worst." Certainly, many of us heed that advice—as do businesses, governments, and corporations—by creating contingency plans. But what happens if everything goes right? It does happen, you know. The best-laid plans come to fruition. You take a risk, and it pays off big-time. That seemingly great person you've met on the dating app turns out to be the love of your life. Are you well equipped to receive and accept the good things that happen to you?

On the surface, that might seem like an odd question. After all, who doesn't want the best to actually happen? However, many of us are stuck in the contingency-plan mindset, and it takes a different mentality to handle better-than-expected outcomes. If you aren't ready to receive those great developments, you may subconsciously reject or sabotage those outcomes to your own detriment. For example, say you apply for a better job with a different employer, but you think it's a long shot. You're offered the role but are racked with doubt, and you take so long to accept it that the offer is ultimately retracted.

The first step to being ready to receive positive outcomes is simply being open to encouraging developments. Then, use your new ability to positively reframe them to find more opportunities and lessons in people, situations, and the world at large. You can also try visualizing the best outcomes, using the vision-board exercise recommended in chapter 3. That's right: just picturing positive results in your mind can make a difference. Researchers from Kings College in London conducted a study with more than one hundred people diagnosed with anxiety disorder. One group was told to visualize an image of a positive outcome to each of the three challenging issues they'd experienced in the previous week, another group was asked to think of verbal positive outcomes, and the last group was asked to visualize any positive image whenever they started to worry. The two groups that visualized positive images—whether related to specific worries or not—reported greater happiness and restfulness, and decreased anxiety.[6]

Embracing hope and joy is another way to reframe your thinking. Hope helps you maintain an optimistic state of mind and makes you more resilient. As reported in the *International Journal of Existential Psychology & Psychotherapy* in 2010, hopeful people find life more meaningful.[7] At the same time, joy, as clinical psychologist Richard Shuster explained to me during our conversation, keeps you in the present moment and adds positive resonance to any experience. Shuster recommends engaging in joy-generating activities on a regular basis, noting that you'll quickly see the benefits of doing so even if you perform them as little as fifteen minutes at a time, a few days a week. "It's impossible to not feel pleasure if you're doing something that you love," he said. "When in that positive state, you're releasing these hormones that are associated with pleasure, like oxytocin and dopamine. What your brain is going to start doing is looking for opportunities to get more of that joy in your environment."

Finally, you can try to adopt a growth mindset, which means that you believe your intelligence and talents can be developed and improved through hard work, strategies, and input from others. Take public speaking, for example. You may lack a natural aptitude or have an initial fear around that activity but recognize that it's an important skill on your road to success. So, you make the commitment to becoming a competent speaker by seeking coaching and joining a group like Toastmasters to practice presenting before others. However, having a fixed mindset means that you believe your smarts and skills cannot be developed—that is, you think that if you aren't good at something like math or cooking, you never will be.

In a January 2016 *Harvard Business Review* article, Carol Dweck, a Stanford University professor and a leading authority on the topic, noted that individuals with a growth mindset "tend to achieve more than those with a more fixed mindset (those who believe their talents are innate gifts). This is because they worry less about looking smart, and they put more energy into learning."[8] This concept is true for individuals and groups, such as those within a corporation. Dweck continued to say that "when entire companies embrace a growth mindset, their employees report feeling far more empowered and committed; they also receive far greater organizational support for collaboration and innovation. In contrast, people at primarily fixed-mindset companies report more of only one thing: cheating and deception among employees, presumably to gain an advantage in the talent race."[9]

Having a growth mindset will help you become more positive because you know that new experiences and different, better results are possible. Rather than going back to previous experiences and focusing on the past—as someone with a fixed mindset is more apt to do—you recognize that things can change when you learn something new and try different approaches. That is true in every aspect of your life—relationships, work, wellness, finances, and more. Having that sense of openness and possibility can encourage you to grow, as well as help you overcome obstacles.

Case Study: McClain Hermes

Famed football coach Lou Holtz once said, "Virtually nothing is impossible in this world if you just put your mind to it and maintain a positive attitude." His words certainly rang true for McClain Hermes. McClain began dreaming about swimming in the Olympics when she was four years old. Around that same time, she started having vision problems that kept getting steadily worse. Finally, at age eight, she was diagnosed with detached retinas in both eyes. McClain underwent three emergency surgeries and then a fourth one within one year. However, she went completely blind in her right eye and was able to barely perceive light and color in her left eye.

When she started to go blind, the first question McClain asked was whether she'd be able to continue swimming. The answer proved to be yes, and she chose to be positive, even when challenges arose. For example, when she was eleven, she attempted to do a flip turn and two laps through the pool, but unfortunately, she couldn't see the wall and kept running into it. That's when it became apparent that a different approach would be needed, so her coaches recommended Paralympic Games swimming. Held in conjunction with and parallel to the Olympics, in the same cities and venues, the Paralympics is an elite series of international, multisport events involving world-class athletes with a range of disabilities. The moment she heard about it, McClain reframed her thinking. Instead of saying "I'll never be able to make the Olympics," she shifted to "I will compete at the Paralympics" and focused on qualifying for the 2016 Paralympic Games in Rio de Janeiro, Brazil.

Making a conscious choice to be positive has kept McClain motivated and focused over the years. "I had two options," she said. "I could have been depressed and sat on the couch eating chips, becoming a fat, grumpy blind person. Or, I could get up and be active and continue to do what I love. Yes, I was given that challenge at age eight, but for me, it was more important to get back in the pool and follow my dreams."

Bolstered by the support of her parents and great coaches, McClain trained hard for the next few years. She made the Paralympics team and competed at the Rio games at age fifteen, even making the finals in the 100-meter backstroke. Choosing to be positive, practicing optimism, looking for the lessons in difficult times, and reframing her thinking when negative thoughts crept in also helped McClain navigate challenges created when the COVID-19 pandemic closed down training facilities and postponed the 2020 Paralympic Games in Tokyo by a year. When she did get to compete in 2021, McClain came in sixth in the women's 400-meter freestyle competition.

McClain's remaining eyesight continues to deteriorate, and she currently competes in the lowest vision class, swimming in blacked-out goggles. "I've been afraid of the dark since I was little and still sleep with my closet light on," she said. "Using totally blacked-out goggles terrified me because what if I go completely blind when I'm swimming, take these goggles off, and then can't see anything. That took a lot of adjusting and mental training for it to be all right. And it's kind of like training my mind and my body to be in total darkness and learn that it's okay."

Being positive and goal oriented continues to be important for McClain these days as she studies communications at Loyola University in Baltimore. Passionate about public speaking, she hopes to inspire others to be positive when challenges come their way by sharing her story of overcoming obstacles.

Case Study: Jennifer Nash, PhD

Jennifer Nash, PhD, didn't realize that being positive was an option when she was growing up. Like many middle-class Midwestern families at the time, her conservative parents were more focused on looking inward, avoiding risk, and preparing for worst-case scenarios.

"It took me a long time to figure out that I can choose to see the positive instead of just focusing on the negatives," explained Jennifer, whose evolution began when she left home for college. Being out in the world, encountering different kinds of people and perspectives while studying abroad, and pursuing a fast-track career shifted her mindset.

"All of that helped me realize that everything isn't so negative," she continued. "I was exposed to different ways of thinking, different ways of being, different cultures, different cuisines, different music, different activities, and extracurriculars in the evenings after work. Those things broadened my horizons in a way that helped me see the good. It allowed me to recognize opportunity and potential, not only for the people around me, but for myself in ways that maybe I hadn't seen before."

Jennifer's former spouse was a glass-half-full kind of person, who further influenced her thinking. For example, when they bought a fixer-upper house, her first thought was about all the work that would be required to make it a great place to live. However, her partner's upbeat attitude helped her ultimately recognize the long-term potential of their home. Things started to fall into place for Jennifer in a better way than they had before, once she deliberately chose a more positive mindset. She said that the first step was self-awareness.

Gaining confidence from a stronger, more positive sense of self prompted Jennifer to obtain an MBA at one of the top business schools in the world. She built an amazing consulting career with one of the Big Four firms and achieved her dream of earning a PhD. Her color palette shifted, as the pastels and soft muted colors that appealed to her growing up were replaced with a strong preference for bold, vivid hues. Preferring the anonymity of team sports growing up, she now gains tremendous joy from shining in the spotlight as a competitive ballroom dancer. Today, Jennifer fully leverages that optimistic mindset in her work as an entrepreneur, a global executive coaching and management consultant, a speaker, and an author.

"Becoming more positive has really helped me center myself in a way that I can then give to others," she added. "The work that I do today recharges me. It helps me be at *my* best so that I can help my clients be at *their* best."

Take Action

Anyone can learn how to increase their level of optimism and choose authentic positivity. Here are some proven practices and steps you can take to reap the benefits of having a more positive outlook:

Action 1: Make a contingency plan for positive outcomes. Although most people think of contingency planning for negative outcomes, you can increase your positive resonance by planning for the best possible scenarios to take place. Let's say you start a side hustle making jewelry that is sold online. Crafting beautiful necklaces and earrings brings you tremendous joy. In fact, you wish that this hobby could produce enough income to become your full-time gig. With that intention set, detail what it looks like when everything falls into place—like sending samples to celebrity stylists for use with their high-profile clients, having luminaries like Beyoncé or Ariana Grande post social media photos of themselves wearing the pieces as a result (generating more than 100,000 likes), and how you plan to handle your production needs when all of the jewelry you've posted on craft sites sells out within days. Think about what your ultimate success story looks like, with you designing a new line of jewelry each season, having full production capabilities in place, and raking in millions of profits. Planning these detailed steps helps make the best possible development more feasible.

Action 2: Ask the Miracle Question. Used by psychologists and coaches, the Miracle Question exercise involves pretending that you've got a magic wand. Ask yourself what would be the one thing that would give you tremendous happiness right now. Perhaps you've struggled with infertility and the thought of becoming a parent fills you with delight. Ignore any inner voices that say this isn't realistic. Discount excuses, and cut through the noise to truly identify what brings you joy. Hope is a natural outcome of the Miracle Question because it forces your brain to really focus on whatever possibility is going to bring you fulfillment and happiness.

Action 3: Practice choosing optimism regularly. Great, so now you've decided to choose positivity. However, this is not a "one and done" type of occurrence. To become more positive in the long term, you need to practice on a daily basis to turn it into a new habit. Martin Seligman created a happiness exercise called "Three Good Things," with a simple premise. Just write down three positive things that happened to you during the day, and reflect on those items at night. Repeat this exercise every day for at least a month. Researchers have found that the longer you do this, the better. The happiness levels of study participants increased by 9 percent after six months of this regular practice.[10]

Action 4: Replace doom-scrolling with uplifting content. Admit it, in recent times, you fell down the rabbit hole of doom-scrolling—you know, obsessively checking your smartphone for updates on the latest news that sends you into a spiral of despair and negativity. Doom-scrolling has a terrible impact on your well-being, but it's increasingly hard to avoid its siren call when it feels like the world has turned sideways. However, a *Washington Post* article from July 2020 reported that you can actually use technology to combat this bad habit by changing your screen display to grayscale to reduce the visual allure, retraining algorithms by clicking on content that covers multiple areas of interest, and using an app to limit screen time. Now, you can fill the void of that negative content with a burst of positivity. Flood your apps, feeds, and content streams with stories about acts of kindness, good people in the world, and uplifting developments. Specific websites like the Optimist Daily and DailyGood specialize in good-news stories, while major media outlets have positive news portals such as Today.com's Good News Section, *USA Today*'s Humankind Section, and CNN's *The Good Stuff* newsletter. Reading that content helps you create a more balanced and ultimately elevated perspective.

Action 5: Look for the lesson. We all have good days and bad. When dealing with a difficult situation, ask yourself what you can learn from that circumstance. When I think back on being diagnosed with Crohn's disease, I learned that no matter what, self-care had to be my top priority. That lesson, and many others from it, continues to help me every day. So make a list of everything learned from your experience, big or small, to reinforce the value gained.

Exercise: Reframe Your Thoughts

Are you ready to start reframing negative thoughts into more positive ones? Here are some steps to take:

Set a baseline. Start noticing how often you have negative thoughts, perhaps marking each instance down on a smart device or notepad. Tally up the number after a week, and you may be surprised by the frequency of this behavior. Consider what circumstances prompted each instance, and identify patterns that are prompting the greatest amount of negative thinking.

Determine what attitude you'd like to change. Looking at the patterns that prompt the greatest amount of negativity, choose one thing to focus on at a time. For example, you might notice a recurring theme of negative thoughts around your relationship with money—how stupid you feel for racking up so much credit card debt, how you're paying too much for your smartphone plan, how you can't afford to renew your apartment lease, frustrations over not having savings for a rainy day, and more.

When a negative thought arises, consider multiple perspectives to find a positive thought. Remember, negative thinking is usually not *accurate*. If overwhelming positivity feels out of reach, choose, instead, to be neutral or realistic. Commonly, we turn to "all or nothing" thinking (words like *always* and *never* are usually used) when things are rarely so black and white. Consider, too, how true this thinking is—is there any evidence to support it? You can also turn negative thoughts into opportunities. Rather than "having" to do something, you can "get" to do something. Instead of giving up when you encounter a roadblock, you can decide to overcome it.

Use the following chart to practice reframing your thoughts. I've filled out the first blocks to help you get started, and I've left the last few blank so you can add your own negative thoughts and the positive reframing for each.

Negative Thought	Positive Reframing
I will never be able to get out of credit card debt.	I am taking accountability for what I owe and am working toward slowly but surely paying it all off.
I know that my boss hated my presentation because she didn't speak with me afterward.	My boss was running late for another meeting after my presentation and left without speaking with anyone. Her busyness is not a reflection of my performance.
I should never have given up our home after the divorce.	Relocating to a new home, where I can discover new things to explore, helped me get over the memories associated with my old home.
My children don't need me anymore.	I'm proud that I've raised independent, healthy kids.
If this next date sucks, I'm going to stop dating.	
I'll never find a job I will enjoy.	
I'm never going to improve my public-speaking skills.	

Negative Thought	Positive Reframing

Practice makes perfect! Run through this cognitive-reframing exercise on a regular basis to retrain your brain. From that place of possibility, you're more apt to get unstuck and create effective solutions.

CHAPTER 9
Pivot with Purpose

Remember the goal you established in chapter 3, the vision for your future state? In this chapter, we're going to use all of the self-discovery and growth work you've completed so far to help you pivot into that desired direction. A pivot involves changing the course of your life for one of three main reasons: when the status quo is no longer working for you, a negative situation forces your hand, or when you simply want to reach for something greater and activate your tremendous potential.

This chapter helps you decide what kind of change you're making: a comeback or a personal transformation. Then you'll explore the benefits of escaping your comfort zone and see how to leverage your strengths and purpose to break your pivot down into smaller, achievable pieces. It's all about creating an action plan for your life that you can then execute.

What It Means to Pivot with Purpose

Pivoting with purpose involves making changes in alignment with your goals, values, and beliefs. Instead of taking a haphazard, reactive approach, your shift in direction is both deliberate and intentional.

A pivot can be broad in nature, involve a specific facet of your being, or take shape as a combination of both. Let's say that in chapter 2, you realized the area in which you're most stuck is being a Debbie Downer. Your pivot could involve developing a more optimistic outlook, which is broader in nature, or it could specifically involve shifting your beliefs about romantic relationships from "I can't meet the right partner" to "I am in a relationship with the right partner, who was worth waiting for," using cognitive reframing, which then propels the actions you'll take to start dating again.

Two subsets of pivoting include making a comeback and pursuing transformation. Within a comeback, you're reemerging from a circumstance that derailed you in some way. A pop-culture example is Tiger Woods. He became a golfing phenomenon, fell from grace during his 2009 scandal, dealt with numerous medical issues, and then rebounded to win the 2019 Masters. I also think of movie star Robert Downey Jr., who garnered an Oscar nomination in 1993 but then spent many of the next few years either in jail or in rehab. He eventually got sober in the early 2000s, focused on his career, and was cast as Ironman, star of the iconic Marvel superhero franchise. However, a comeback doesn't have to involve rebounding from dramatic events, as these two celebrities did. You might be planning how to rise above a smaller, though still significant, disappointment, such as getting rejected from law school or not landing any of the acting roles you auditioned for this year.

A comeback is about restoring your personal stature to the level you once held—or exceeding it with new accomplishments and milestones. People who make comebacks rise above their stuckness and setbacks to surge forward in a familiar manner.

However, when it comes to pursuing the second type of pivot—a transformation—that can involve blazing a different or entirely new path. I define *transformation* as the process of honestly assessing what works for you now, jettisoning what doesn't, being open to change, and exploring new directions that can yield great fulfillment and happiness. The key is staying true to yourself. That's why you took the time to identify your desired future state in chapter 3 and gained greater self-awareness using the tools in chapter 4. You have to understand your goals, purpose, values, and strengths first in order to act in alignment with them as you move forward.

Comedian and actor George Lopez once said, "When things are bad, it's the best time to reinvent yourself." His point may be right on the money. If you're feeling stuck, that kind of change can present a good opportunity to recalibrate who you are and how you present yourself to the world. However, reinvention doesn't have to be prompted by negative circumstances. You might identify an opportunity to make an already good life more vibrant. Perhaps you've been pigeon-holed into one profession while there's an opportunity to take it to the next level in another way. To draw from pop culture again, that's what singer Jessica Simpson did, who is now better known for building a billion-dollar fashion company than for her music; as well as Steve Harvey, who parlayed his career in comedy into an entertainment empire that includes TV shows, books, speaking engagements, and multiple businesses.

With this understanding, determine if you're making a comeback or pursuing personal transformation. Either way, that kind of change and growth isn't possible when you're stuck deep within your comfort zone. Management consultant and author Judith Bardwick coined the phrase *comfort zone* more than thirty years ago to describe "a behavioral state within which a person operates in an anxiety-neutral condition, using a limited set of behaviors to deliver a steady level of performance, usually without a sense of risk."[1] A comfort zone, without any challenges or risks, is a narrow place to be—sure, you're safe and relaxed, but there isn't a lot of incentive to shake things up, pursue personal growth, or achieve outstanding results. Things will stay the same because *you* do.

However, there are numerous benefits to breaking out of your comfort zone. As leadership strategist and personal mastery expert Shadé Zahrai noted, they include becoming more productive, increasing adaptability to change, enhancing creativity, and promoting personal growth.[2] In order to successfully pivot, you often need to step outside of your comfort zone in order to see what's possible, gain new ideas, test your limits, and take calculated risks. Of course, leaving a comfort zone can be quite a challenge. Many people face psychological roadblocks, which can range from a fear of being authentic or disliked to worries about lacking the competence to do so. No wonder they opt to stay in a narrow place of perceived safety, like lying in bed underneath a pile of blankets. Contained and comforting at first, it can become suffocating and limiting as time goes on. So let's talk more about proven strategies to help you break out of *your* comfort zone.

Andy Molinsky, PhD, the author of *Reach: A New Strategy to Help You Step Outside Your Comfort Zone, Rise to the Challenge, and Build Confidence*, told me that he advises people to employ four key concepts to escape that place of self-imposed limits. The first is conviction, which is the sense of purpose you identified in chapter 4. The second is customization, which involves tweaking a situation to encourage you to take action. Confronting something outside of your comfort zone can trigger some intense emotions like fear and distorted thinking, so the third step is clarity, the ability to see things as they actually are to normalize reactions and have more evenhanded emotional responses. Fourth, then, is taking a leap, where you try out a situation and discover that it wasn't as difficult as you first perceived it.

Molinsky recommends building your courage through repetition to make your comfort-zone escape stick. The key is to start with doable tasks that generate small wins and then continue to stretch in further increments. For example, most athletes who want to train for a marathon start running a few miles a day, build up their strength, and then increase to longer distances before eventually being able to handle all twenty-six miles. The same applies to other situations that require a certain level of discomfort.

Okay, that's the plan for leaving your comfort zone. Once you're fully open to change and taking risks, you can start to pivot in earnest. The next step is to leverage your strengths and purpose, as you identified in chapter 4, in alignment with how you wish to get unstuck, in order to break your pivot down into smaller, achievable pieces.

Take a moment to recall the strengths you identified in chapter 4. A successful pivot is often based on recognizing what you do well and refocusing it in a new way. Let's pause to pull all of these elements together. By way of example, let's say that the area you defined as your greatest area of stuckness is not trusting yourself; you live in a bustling metropolis because that's what people thought you should do after college, and it doesn't reflect what you actually desire anymore. Living in a big, expensive city hundreds of miles away from other family members has become a major source of frustration. In chapter 4, you defined your purpose as building a happy family unit, which you could accomplish by seeing your children thrive and experiencing a fulfilling relationship with your significant other. When you identified your strengths, two that top the list are forming close relationships and solving problems. In fact, those two factors have allowed you to succeed in many areas, including your career when remote working became the norm and you had to juggle virtual meetings while educating your preteens at home. That brings us to the pivot you desire, which is to leave the big city and relocate to a smaller town closer to family and friends. Great—that part is clear. But you can't just leave it big and open-ended. Successfully navigating a pivot involves breaking all of its components down into manageable steps.

List everything that you'll need to do in order to crush this pivot. In this example, it might include details like where you'd like to move, whether you keep your current job in a remote working arrangement or do something different, checking out local schools for your kids, researching the housing market in target communities, and more. Your strengths in forming relationships and solving problems will allow you to tackle all of these items well, and advance planning ensures that you think through as much as possible before pursuing this pivot.

You may be prompted to change now based on getting unstuck. But after learning how to pivot, these same strategies can be used anytime you want to more toward to a new, more fulfilling place. With the right focus and proven tools, people can come back from any setback or transform themselves however and whenever they like. Okay, right now you might be thinking that it may be too late for you or that you've been stuck too long. That simply isn't true. Consider the story of Anne Dowsett Johnston.

Case Study: Anne Dowsett Johnston

You can reinvent yourself at any age. Just ask Ann Dowsett Johnston, an award-winning journalist and bestselling author who went back to college in her sixties to become a psychotherapist. Ann spent twenty-five years working for *Maclean's* magazine, Canada's leading newsweekly, while raising a young son as a single mother. The Toronto resident then became the vice principal of McGill University in her midfifties. However, it was a difficult time, as she hit a huge depression tied to empty nest syndrome, menopause, and handling a demanding job that wasn't a fit for her creative interests—all while juggling life as a high-functioning alcoholic.

Ann left her role at the university to take care of herself, and achieved sobriety with the help of rehab. She won a $100,000 fellowship to look at how the alcohol industry pitched women around the world. That work became the basis for her 2013 critically acclaimed bestseller *Drink: The Intimate Relationship Between Women and Alcohol*. Ann's personal story and efforts to destigmatize mental health and addiction resonated with millions of people through her writing and a popular TEDx talk.

Then, Ann decided to fulfill a decades-old dream of becoming a psychotherapist. She ignored naysayers who questioned her age and ploughed through the challenges, graduating with a master's degree in social work at the age of sixty-five. The reinvention continues. Today, at age sixty-eight, Ann leads a successful business called Writing Your Recovery, an online learning course about the healing power of writing memoirs.

"It takes gumption, and for me, it also took the death of my parents to realize that life is finite," Ann explained. "I'm a big believer now in if you see something in life, you need to seize it rather than postpone it. Be prepared to be surprised by life. My experience is that God has a better imagination than I do. I'm constantly surprised at how remarkable life is, expanding like an accordion to offer us chances that are rich."

Case Study: Dorie Clark

Dorie Clark, whom we already met in chapter 2, became adept at pivoting early in her career. Twenty years ago, as a young political reporter working in Boston, she was laid off during a round of cutbacks. She planned to start looking for a new job the next day, which was September 11, 2001. Needless to say, things didn't go as planned. Dorie wanted to stay in journalism, but with the recession and economic standstill following the terrorist attack, no one was hiring. She scraped by as a freelancer, but it was hard.

About six months later, she was offered a job as the press secretary for a governor's race. She was resistant at first but then changed her mind. This became the first of many career-defining pivots. Dorie ended up moving from journalism and political communications to serving as a nonprofit's executive director. However, she craved the autonomy of working for herself and making a difference on her own terms. In 2006, she pivoted with purpose into entrepreneurship.

Dorie wrote best-selling books about branding and reinvention and delivered speeches around the world. Teaching executive education at

Duke University's Fuqua School of Business and Columbia Business School, she also consulted for major corporations; did executive coaching at the individual level; and ran online courses, in-person workshops, and yearlong mastermind groups.

When the COVID-19 pandemic struck, it wasn't business as usual, as travel came to a standstill. Dorie was used to being on the road 50 percent of the time delivering presentations and keynote speeches. In April 2020 alone, she was scheduled to speak in Russia, Egypt, Texas, Virginia, and British Columbia, but all of these engagements were canceled. Concerned that her income would grind to a halt, Dorie decided that it was time to pivot with purpose again into a state of being she'd been planning for years—to travel less, be more connected to others in her life, and generate income streams that weren't solely dependent on physically delivering services or traveling to events.

That advance thinking paid off. Dorie refocused her efforts into online course offerings. She created courses with LinkedIn Learning and relaunched her Recognized Expert course six months earlier than planned. She wrote her next book, *The Long Game: How to Be a Long-Term Thinker in a Short-Term World*, fully explored her interest in musical theater, and spent more time with friends and family. Her business and quality of life continue to thrive now in new and different ways because of her intentional pivot.

Take Action

If *you* are ready to pivot, here are some steps to help you accomplish that with purpose:

Action 1: Decide if you're pursuing a comeback or a transformation. Are you looking to reemerge from a setback in a familiar manner, which would be a comeback; or more comprehensively transform, which could involve a completely different path? Understand which kind of pivot you're seeking at this time. Determining the scope of your pivot is essential in effectively planning it.

Action 2: Make sure that your pivot is based on purpose. Refer back to your purpose statement from chapter 4. Jot down how you're stuck, your desired state, and your strengths, and use this information to help you plan a pivot that is in full alignment with those factors.

Action 3: Use the 5 ws. Plan your pivot by answering what is called the "5 *ws*" in writing: *who, what, when, where,* and *why*. Starting with these interrogative questions lets you break down all of the details that you need to consider when successfully pivoting.

Action 4: Use verbal reinforcement. The spoken word can be incredibly powerful. Stating the intentions behind your pivot out loud can bring them to life, help you get unstuck, and reach new heights of success. That's what Mike Bean did when considering a career transformation in the form of leaving a financial planning firm to start his own practice. He set clear goals for his new firm and then said them out loud daily. During the first year, business was up 45 percent over his previous practice, and it more than tripled in the next five years. His pivot became even more rewarding and successful through this practice.

Exercise: Create Your Comeback Action Plan

In addition to being an executive coach, author, and speaker, one of my areas of expertise is communications strategy and brand image development. I've spent nearly thirty years helping numerous organizations and people reach breakout status, deal with crisis situations, and navigate a combination of both.

Below is a template that I initially developed to launch new corporate initiatives, detailing thinking about proposed projects in order to gain alignment with all approving parties. I sound a bit more corporate even explaining it here, right? Then I realized that the process of thinking through all of the parts of a process or project in this manner would help people soar personally as well.

I'm going to use a career-based example for the purposes of this template. Let's say that you became a stay-at-home parent and are now ready to return to the workforce after a prolonged absence. See how your responses could appear in this scenario throughout the template.

Following are the components you will complete:

Situation Analysis/Overview

In this section, you'll define your current circumstances. Answer the following questions to create your overview, which essentially is a story about what happened and how you plan to move forward.

What circumstances have led me to this point? What happened? It could be: *I was a human resources manager who decided to stay home permanently after giving birth to my second child. While lucky to be in a financial position to do so, I ended up putting everyone else's needs above my own. With my children now in high school, I'm ready to return to the workforce.*

Why do I want to make a comeback? *I miss having adult conversations each day and could use a regular paycheck as we save to put the kids through college. I also want to use my skills and intelligence to thrive in a positive work environment.*

What does that comeback look like? *Human resources is a field I really enjoyed. I'd like to find a job with a nearby company that lets me work remotely several days a week.*

What is my niche? (Be specific in this point.) *Within Human Resources, I really enjoy recruiting and benefits, which are two areas that are in high demand.*

How does this align with my purpose, values, and strengths? *I care about helping others and value creating engaging environments, whether that is for employees, family, or friends. This aligns with my purpose of making a positive difference by being of service to other people.*

Objectives

Here, you'll list your specific goals in bullet format. In the case of making a career comeback, it could look something like this:

- Find a human resources generalist job with a company I like, close to home.
- Maintain flexibility by working from home at least three days a week.
- Do work each day that brings me fulfillment and fair compensation.

Target Audiences

List everyone whom you'd need to influence and/or work with to make a successful comeback. In this case, it could include:

- Prospective employers—describe what that encompasses—types of industries, areas of specialties, number of employees, and more.
- Professional network—people who can give you career advice, refer you to opportunities, and support your job search.

Key Tactics

Here, you'll list everything you need to do in order to make your comeback successful. A few starter areas to consider in this career comeback example include:

- **Update your résumé.** Use current formats and keywords that will pass electronic screening systems.
- **Utilize social media.** Build a professional profile on LinkedIn that highlights your expertise and any related activities you've done while raising a family, which will enhance the job search.
- **Brush up on your skills.** Determine which industry certifications or knowledge in specific programs can help you land your next job, and take the relevant courses or read applicable books.
- **Network.** Reach out to individuals you've identified as sources of help to request advice and connections while approaching new contacts who could be willing to offer assistance.

This is a living document. Although it might be used to plan over a six-month, annual, or multiyear period, you can update it at any time as circumstances and opportunities evolve. I hope this template will serve as a helpful road map for your comeback!

CHAPTER 10

Build a Support System

As you pivot with purpose, keep in mind that you don't need to go it alone. In fact, being isolated and not having a healthy community to lean on is one of the common ways in which people get stuck (see chapter 2). Isolation may not be your primary roadblock, but everyone can benefit from assessing their support system and making sure it's as valuable as possible. As you raise your game or adopt new behaviors, it's helpful to gather a positive system of support to encourage you when times get tough.

Kudos on completing all of the work you've done up till now to get clear about who you are, what you want, and how you're going to get there. In this chapter, you'll learn how to make all of those lessons and plans stronger by garnering support from like-minded souls, finding camaraderie, and seeking help from professionals, if needed. We'll also cover the importance of giving support to others.

What It Means to Build a Support System

A support system comprises the people you can count on to have your back and act in accordance with your best interests. It can involve a community of individuals who share common concerns, your friends, a family group, or the one you create. It may be a religious, educational, or civic organization. Your community could also take the form of a formal support group or multistep program that promotes healing or dealing with loss. Or, it may constitute a gathering of people who are united in their passion for a topic, such as vegan cooking or maintaining a healthy life after they quit smoking. Within this kind of construct, individuals come together to share their feelings, concerns, setbacks, and milestones, looking to receive and share both support and validation from others who have gone through similar circumstances.

Research has shown that receiving positive social support improves your overall well-being. In a 2007 article in *Psychiatry Journal* called "Social Support and Resilience to Stress," the authors concluded that "social support is exceptionally important for maintaining good physical and mental health. Overall, it appears that positive social support of high quality can enhance resilience to stress, help protect against developing trauma-related psychopathology, decrease the functional consequences of trauma-induced disorders, such as post-traumatic stress disorder (PTSD), and reduce medical morbidity and mortality."[1] The Mayo Clinic also notes the benefit of a positive social group, such as gaining empowerment and hope; feeling less isolated or judged; increasing motivation and coping skills; reducing stress, depression, and anxiety; and gaining access to practical feedback and resources.[2]

You may consider seeking professional help as part of this mix. Turning to certified, credentialed therapists, coaches, counselors, and spiritual leaders can make a big difference as you get unstuck and achieve your desired state of being. Mental Health America, a leading nonprofit advocacy group, notes that mental health professionals can help people come up with plans for solving problems, feel stronger in the face of challenges, change behaviors that hold them back, gain different perspectives, heal past pains, determine goals, and build more self-confidence. This kind of support can assist you in increasing your commitment to emotional and physical wellness, removing obstacles, and dealing with changes at different stages of life, like coping with divorce, menopause, grief, and your shifting role as a parent or caregiver. The organization reports that most people who seek help feel better, citing that more than 80 percent of people treated for depression improve, and treatment for panic disorders shows up to a 90 percent success rate.[3]

It's also valuable to belong to multiple supportive communities. Personally, I've benefited from numerous sources of support. In terms of professional help, I saw a fantastic therapist years ago who helped me create a positive relationship with myself; and these days, I have an excellent executive coach who provides guidance as I overcome obstacles and reach for more. As I finalize this book, I've got my core friend group, an online community of peers who share a love of fitness, fellow certified coaches who also get completely geeky about human potential, and a number of recognized experts who are developing their thought-leadership expertise.

The truth is, we grow and evolve more through healthy connections with others. Being part of a community is practically wired into our DNA, going back to when it really did take a village for people to hunt, gather food, create shelter, and be there for each other just to survive. Beyond that baseline, we need positive relationships with others in order to thrive and get unstuck. S. D. Shanti, DDS, MPH, PhD, CPH, a psychologist, public health professional, and the founder of Prescriptions for Hope, a Swiss nonprofit foundation, found this to be true in her work. "The fundamental nature of what it means to be human is that we grow up and survive in connection with other people. Without that connection, it's difficult to thrive and realize one's gifts," she told me. "Connection comes in many different forms beyond romantic relationships or close friendships. It's teachers caring about students. Neighbors looking out for one another. That's at the core of what we are as human beings."

Forming positive connections with others can change the course of your life. Emmy Werner, PhD, conducted the groundbreaking Kauai Longitudinal Study in Hawaii from the 1950s through the 1970s. She looked at the developmental trajectory of children born into "high risk" families to determine if they would have an increased probability of developing mental health problems later in life. The presence of emotional support was key; kids born with chronic conditions at birth who didn't have this type of support were seven times more likely to develop minimal brain dysfunctions than similar children who had adequate support. In the course of that study, the researchers discovered that not everybody who grew up in a difficult family setting ended up having challenges, and that many children demonstrated the potential for positive change and growth. The difference was personal resilience, a critical element being a healthy connection with another person who didn't have to be in one's immediate family.[4] For example, that connection could have come from a teacher, an extended family member, or a loving caretaker.

"Connection with other people is integral to our sense of well-being," added Shanti. "Because it also feeds into our need for meaning in our lives. That's what allows interactions to be transcendental rather than just transactional."

One of the longest-running studies of adult life in the world, the eighty-plus-year-old Harvard Study of Adult Development, supports Shanti's perspective. The study has shown that embracing community improves the quality and longevity of your life. In tracking participant issues in health, careers, personal life, and more, the research team found that having positive relationships significantly impacts your well-being. "The surprising finding is that our relationships and how happy we are in our relationships has a powerful influence on our health," said Robert Waldinger, MD, the director of the study, a psychiatrist at Massachusetts General Hospital, and a professor of psychiatry at Harvard Medical School. "Taking care of your body is important, but tending to your relationships is a form of self-care, too. That, I think, is the revelation."[5]

Let's talk about how you find the right community for your needs. Start by considering your goals. Do you hope to find solutions from other people who have been stuck in a similar manner, or to get support when you feel yourself slipping into self-sabotaging behaviors? For example, members of the online private fitness group I belong to provide encouragement for each other when it comes to exercise and healthy living; we check in regularly to record our workouts to give each other support and accountability.

Next, think about timing parameters. Is spending an hour at a weekly therapy session all that you've got the capacity for at this point? Or would you like to gain ongoing support as needed in another manner? Plan in advance how many hours you're willing to allocate each week or month on your journey toward getting unstuck.

Then consider how you'd like your support system to take shape and form. Do you prefer in-person, online, or a hybrid of both? These days, just about any type of interaction—therapy sessions, support-group meetings, conferences, and more—can take place virtually, so geography doesn't have to be a barrier. (You'll see more tips in the Take Action section on how to find and connect with new sources of support.)

Also, make sure you determine if the time spent with this kind of support system is beneficial. Given our busy lives, there's no reason to waste hours on an experience that isn't delivering what you need. I'm lucky enough to receive a lot of invitations for groups that sound interesting, but I simply don't have the time to participate. So, it takes a lot for me to make a commitment. And when I do commit, the experience has to be fulfilling, like it is with the online fitness group I mentioned earlier. Most of the people in that group are scattered throughout the United States, Canada, the United Kingdom, Europe, and Asia, so I've only met a few in person. That doesn't matter, though. I've formed friendships with wonderful birds of a feather who provide me with support and smart tips about wellness. It helps me stay motivated, even when I'm just checking in to be an active cheerleader for others. I visit that site every other day or so, even when I'm slammed with other commitments.

Remember, it's fine to change things up as needed. It took me three attempts to find the right therapist decades ago. There's nothing wrong with trying a resource and then ditching it immediately, or after a short-time period, if you don't receive the anticipated level of support. Support groups that could have been invaluable to you at first may no longer work on a longer-term basis, as you continue to evolve. Keep things fresh by making changes as you grow. Today, you might join a weight-loss support group for avowed couch potatoes, and then two years from now, with different goals, you may find yourself leading a community of people who are passionate about competitive weight lifting.

When establishing a community, it's also important to realize that you may need to directly ask for support, which isn't always easy to do. You might beat yourself up initially, thinking that you should resolve a problem or task on your own without help from others. But that's not doing yourself any favors. No one knows everything, and collective brainpower can be so much more effective than going it alone. Receiving input from others can expand your thinking and present new alternatives for solving problems. It decreases the burden of trying to solve issues by yourself. Taking a break from solitary stress allows you to gain more clarity; plus, it can actually help you build better relationships with others.

Sherri W. Fisher, director of Learn & Flourish and the author of *The Effort Myth: How to Give Your Child the Gift of Motivation*, observed this as well during our conversation. "When you only reach inward, you may find that you're far more capable than you ever could have imagined. You also put yourself at risk for burnout, which can be difficult to repair," she noted. "It's good to turn toward people, so they know that you do depend on them and that you value their expertise. People want to use their strengths. Asking for support is a relationship builder."

Another relationship builder is supporting others. I'm assuming that you've heard the message at some point that it's better to give than receive. Personally, I don't think that giving and receiving should be an either/or proposition; people tend to be better off when they do plenty of both. But what you might not realize is that being there for others doesn't just benefit them. Helping others can go a long way toward improving your ability to overcome obstacles while promoting personal growth.

A study published in *Psychosomatic Medicine: Journal of Biobehavioral Medicine* in 2016 suggests that giving support may be as important as being open to receiving it in terms of improving your health. Researchers found that giving support to others can have a positive impact on the parts of your brain involved in stress, reward, and caregiving activities. They saw this behavior as possibly improving health by reducing activity in the stress- and threat-related regions of your mind during stressful experiences.[6] "It's a very well-established phenomenon that helping helps the helper," noted Ludmila N. Praslova, PhD, who also spoke to me on the topic of resilience. "Multiple studies have shown that it improves mood, increases our sense of agency, and helps us thrive. When you're helping someone, not only you are in control of your reality, but you are helping to change someone else's."

Asking for support and help—and giving it to others in return—is essential in helping you get unstuck and effectively pivot. Think about the pivoting action-plan exercise you completed in the previous chapter. Whether you're looking to make a comeback or a transformation, much of your success will depend on getting assistance from others. You need honest, open feedback from those you trust. The ability to ask others for help is critical, whether your intention is to build professional connections as you return to the workforce or learn how to love again following a brutal divorce. Be clear about the help you need and the trusted people you can turn to, and refer back to the tips mentioned in this chapter to find the right community for you. Get started by taking one step at a time.

As noted earlier, supporting others can help you heal and grow—so please don't overlook this step. I think about Jenny Lisk, who was consumed by grief when her husband died from brain cancer, leaving her as a young widow with two small children. She received great support from professionals, family, and friends but couldn't find a lot of information on what to expect as a widowed parent. So Lisk created *The Widowed Parent* podcast to help others by sharing her perspective as a layperson who has lived it herself and can relate to the experiences of listeners. Then she published a critically acclaimed book called *Future Widow: Losing My Husband, Saving My Family, and Finding My Voice*. Being a helpful resource has been healing and meaningful for Lisk as she moves forward in life.

Case Study: Anne Buckingham

Anne Buckingham's support system comprises great people from an international rowing community that spans two continents. The group is heavily, but not exclusively, male. What they have in common is a love for the sport, a strong sense of decency, and a commitment to supporting each other during the best and worst of times.

Briefly exposed to rowing while studying in England, Anne decided to take classes at Community Rowing, Inc., in Boston as a way to meet new people when she relocated to the city. She fell in love with the sport and soon found herself biking there eight miles most mornings so she could row before daybreak, before heading off to her job and then attending law school at night. Upon receiving an email asking for volunteers for the prestigious head of the Charles Regatta, Anne was happy to help. When organizers learned that she is 6'5", they asked her to be in charge of the dock where boats launched and landed. Three years later when Anne wound up giving a crew the first unsportsmanlike-conduct penalty for conduct on the dock before they even launched, the impressed planning team made her an umpire for the event.

When asked what being part of this group has given her, Anne replied, "Everything. Being a volunteer has enabled an exceptionally shy person to talk to people and meet them because you have a job to do. And then you find your tribe and you build your network."

Today, Anne lives in the UK and has been called the "Kevin Bacon of rowing," because as a result of her many years of volunteerism, if she doesn't know someone personally, it's only a degree or two of separation before she does. She expanded her regatta duties to serve as an umpire, ombudsman, commentator, and liaison for international elite athletes over her twenty-three years of service. Anne volunteered at the 2012 Paralympics Games in London, became an assistant to the British para-rowing team, and volunteered for the World Coastal Rowing Championships in Vancouver in 2018. She also serves as the crew liaison for Henley Women's and Henley Masters Regattas, sourcing housing, boats, and transport, and assisting with logistics for overseas competitors. In addition, she sits on the board for a prominent rowing club. All of this constitutes a large, time-intensive commitment, but Anne says that it has made her a better mother, lawyer, and human being, and she wouldn't be who she was without it.

That became even more evident following a series of traumatic events in Anne's life. Between February and March 2020, she left a company that didn't share her same level of ethics; and her husband suddenly died unexpectedly, leaving her as a single parent to their eight-year-old daughter. Weeks later, the global pandemic fully hit the UK, shutting everything down.

Anne's tribe sprang into action. Friends dropped off meals and desserts, and the worldwide rowing community sent flowers and thoughtful messages. Buddies started an entire WhatsApp group chat that she's never seen, where they coordinated support for her. She trained with everyone on erg machines in her backyard when boathouses shut down, and one friend appointed herself as the person to take Anne out for margaritas when the initial wave of lockdowns lifted. She even had two student athletes living in her home who have pitched in to help with daily tasks.

Explaining this outpouring of support, Anne said, "It's natural that you'll lean on some people more than others and rely on individuals for certain things. People reached out who I don't even know."

Case Study: Qing Li

Qing Li is part of two distinctive communities that continue to make a positive difference in her world. While she was a student at MIT, she swam the English Channel. "I was struggling a bit in the first couple of years going into an elite school, where everyone around me was curing cancer or starting start-ups, or whatever," she said, reflecting on the pressure to be perfect while constantly comparing herself to others. "So I saw the English Channel as an opportunity for me to do my thing."

To offer some context, swimming the English Channel is like climbing Mt. Everest for open-water swimmers. Years of training and preparation can be required to swim the dangerous, frigid waters; and fewer than two thousand people have completed the solo swim. Talk about an incredible achievement! However, after she completed her goal, Qing recalled having a sense of "Well, is this it?"

She started tackling other big goals, such as obtaining a master's degree. Burned out from swimming, Qing completely stopped engaging in the sport while starting her career path. However, something was missing. She was working at a consulting job that required extensive travel, and she started engaging in stints of heavy drinking and extravagant spending. It felt like a lot of mental health issues came to a head, and everything was falling apart. "I realized that my lifestyle wasn't healthy, and I needed to make a change," Qing said. "And what really caused me to rethink a lot of things was the overwhelming feeling of being alone in the world. That every issue out there somehow fell on my shoulders, and I had no one to talk to about those issues."

After a six-year hiatus, Qing realized that the swimming community could offer tremendous support. She decided to continue her pursuit of the open-water Triple Crown, which is swimming the English Channel, as she had already done; swimming around Manhattan Island; and swimming the Catalina Channel, which goes from Catalina Island to Los Angeles. It became part of a larger shift in her life. "When I came back into open-water swimming, that community provided me with support and modeled a lot of the values, virtues, and good behaviors that I wanted to instill in myself," she explained. "Even when you're leading the charge on social issues or putting positivity out into the world, there are still bad days. You can acknowledge the facts of that day and what might be really painful—but you can also see the positive, opportunity, and your values."

Qing spiraled into a dark place, just as millions of people worldwide did, when the COVID-19 pandemic occurred. A few weeks earlier, she'd felt elated after participating in an open-water swim fundraiser in Sierra Leone, one of the poorest countries in the world. She returned to Chicago just as COVID-19 was starting to spread in the United States. "When we first went into the shutdown, I basically had a psychotic break of sorts," she explained. "It wasn't as bad as several years ago, but it was a really, really tough time for me because I'd spent the last several years building those support pillars in my life and didn't want to ever feel alone again."

A friend who lived nearby proved to be a saving grace, meeting her for early-morning walks to see the sunrise and engage in human interaction. Dissatisfied with her career, Qing felt a sense of relief when her job was eliminated a few months later. With all of the changes, the open-water swimming community remained a constant source of support. "These people are amazing human beings, and they are my role models in every aspect. I'm connected with them on Facebook and other virtual means, and I know they're always there for me," said Qing. "Community doesn't have to be the physical place you live. Rather, it is those people you engage with on a day-to-day basis, whom you lean on when things are tough, and who also share positive things as well."

Recently, Qing joined another organization related to her heritage and career development called the National Association of Asian American Professionals. "I've found another professional network community where they're of my skin color," she said. "I'm starting to bridge that gap of feeling like myself and having fun while also getting back into the professional world. With the power of having people help you, you can actually do more awesome, bigger things with that support," she added.

Take Action

Are you ready to get more support as you pivot with purpose? Start with the action steps listed below. Building a healthy support system is a two-way street. In order to get the most out of this process, you've got to find the right community for your needs and be willing to help others in return.

> **Action 1: Identify the kind of support you need.** Think about the desired outcome for your pivot. Let's say that your doctor has diagnosed you as morbidly obese and you're concerned as well after finding yourself out of breath after climbing a flight of stairs or walking more than a block. Your intended pivot is improving personal wellness, and you plan to accomplish it by moving more and eating healthier. Now be as specific as possible in identifying the support needed to achieve your goals. Can you accomplish this with minimal support, like apps or guided videos—or do you need regular human interaction or training to build accountability? Lean into the work you did to understand who you are to determine this; for example, an extrovert will get more motivation out of walking with a friend or taking a group exercise class than sitting on an exercise bike alone.
>
> **Action 2: Assess your current levels of support.** With your clarity about the kind of support you need, determine which resources are currently accessible. Make a list of the people in

your life who can offer help with your pivot. Different individuals can bring many things to the table. For example, if you're looking to make a career shift, think about friends who are well connected within your desired industry, or LinkedIn connections. Ask them for introductions to prospective employers. Cast a wide net as you consider the people you already know who would be delighted to help. That buddy of yours who always knows what to wear to any occasion can help you plan a great interview outfit that helps you look and feel confident in person or during a video call. Or perhaps your cousin's college roommate is now a hiring manager for a company you'd love to work for, and this person would be happy to hook you up for a conversation.

Action 3: Practice asking for help. Asking someone else for help doesn't come easily for most of us. But as you've learned in this chapter, being of service to others often makes people feel better about themselves. Don't automatically assume that your request might be an imposition. There are a few tips to keep in mind to make your "ask" as effective as possible. Be flexible, cordial, and direct. Rather than saying, "You seem interesting—can we meet for coffee and talk sometime so I can get advice?," be specific. I'll use the career example again here. It's more effective to state your circumstance ("I'm looking for a new job in communications that focuses on employee engagement"), explain why you're approaching that person ("I'm impressed with your award-winning work in this area"), and specify the request ("Can you spare fifteen to twenty minutes to review my résumé and share advice?"). Then, demonstrate your flexibility ("I'm available to meet anytime that works for your schedule over the next month"). Here's where the cordial part comes in: thank them for considering your request and mention that you'd love to be of service to them in the future—and mean it.

Practice writing this request, keeping it to just a few sentences, until it sounds polished. Proofread it carefully before sending your note to that individual via a social media platform, email, or text. Keep in mind that some people, no matter how well intentioned, might simply be too busy to help, and you may not hear back from them. Don't badger people with multiple follow-ups, especially if you've never met them before. Just let it go and see who else might be of assistance. Eventually, the right individuals will be able to offer you the help you seek.

Action 4: Find a new community. The people you currently know may not be able to offer the kind of support you require, prompting you to search for a new community. I've found that the easiest way to locate like-minded souls is to search online for groups that reflect your passions or needs. All of that great work you did to identify your purpose, strengths, and values comes into play now as you look for others who've walked in your shoes and can offer insights on solving problems.

Let's say you have a burning desire to connect with other perimenopausal women who are experiencing empty-nest syndrome as their kids leave home for college. Facebook is a great place to start seeking established groups, especially where a moderator acts as a gatekeeper to approve your acceptance into the community, which establishes a level of quality control. If you've read a book on perimenopause or empty-nest syndrome that strongly resonates with you, check to see if the author has a community of supporters to engage with. Consider checking out other groups you belong to that may cover those topics, such as fellow parents of students graduating high school, the subdivision where you reside, or a fellowship group at your house of worship. Just remember to be authentic to yourself and choose a community that is focused on support rather than put-downs and snarky comments.

Action 5: Make a commitment. Learn what is required to become part of the community you're considering. If you join a support group that requires in-person sessions three times a week, show up as planned. When the guidelines of an online group ask for daily comments, be one of the first to comply. Honoring those requirements will allow you and your fellow participants to get the most out of the process.

Action 6: Find ways to help others. As mentioned earlier, being a source of support is great for your well-being. Wondering how to be of service to others? Think about how you act when attending a dinner party at a friend's house. As a gracious guest, you might bring a gift, offer to help upon arriving, and assist with cleanup without being asked. It's about actively anticipating the needs of others. The same applies when you're a member of a support system. Going back to the example of perimenopausal women who are becoming empty-nesters, you might proactively answer the questions of parents whose kids are leaving home for the first time, since you lived through that circumstance several years ago. Or it may involve offering encouragement when others seem to be struggling, posting about what you've learned from your experiences, and more. Anticipate what people might need, and offer to help; chances are good that they'll do the same for you.

Exercise: Identify Your Ideal Support System

This chapter contains a lot of practical steps about how to join or create a support system. However, you also need to trust your instincts in creating the ideal support for your needs. Answering the thinking prompts that follow will help you understand what type of support—within a group, from friends, or from professionals—resonates the strongest with who you are today:

1. When was the last time you felt truly supported? Describe the circumstance and the people who were most helpful.

2. Make a list of all of the communities you've been part of in your life. Note everything that made a significant impact on you, going back as far as needed. For example, being a member of your high school marching band might still conjure up numerous great memories, while the friends you made of fellow parents from your kid's preschool play group may offer tremendous support twenty years later.

3. Pick the two to four most positive experiences. Consider what made them so beneficial for you. What did these communities bring to you? What did you contribute to them?

4. Look at your notes and pinpoint what these best experiences had in common. Was it being united around a common cause, or being surrounded by others who truly had your back?

5. How can you create a similar positive resonance around an experience now? Use these responses as your guidelines to identify the ideal support for your desired pivot and journey in order to stay unstuck moving forward.

Part Four

Maintaining Your New Trajectory

CHAPTER 11

Prioritize Wellness

It is time for some self-acknowledgment. At this point, you've identified how you're most stuck and have taken a pause to gain clarity about your desired state. You've kept up that positive momentum by doing all of the Take Action exercises, including identifying your values and strengths to find your purpose, building trust and confidence in yourself, and giving yourself permission to change and get unstuck. When it came time to taking action, you crushed learning how to become more resilient, actively chose optimism, pivoted with purpose, and built a support system to sustain your goals. I'm sending you a huge round of applause right now for getting yourself unstuck.

Now, this section is going to focus on reinforcing all the great results you've generated. Because even if you *have* achieved your goals at this point, it's not uncommon to stumble or start to slip. What matters in those moments is taking swift action to get right back on track. The following chapters focus on helping you maintain your positive trajectory, reduce the risk of backsliding, and build additional skills to make a quick course correction if needed.

One effective way to do so is to prioritize wellness. Sure, people know intellectually that taking care of their well-being is important. But when it comes to actually doing it, the same individuals who would never miss a smart-device update and always clean the lint screen on their dryers can push personal wellness to the back burner without a second thought. That can happen when people view self-care as "selfish." But self-care is important to practice even when times are good. If you don't, you won't be your strongest self when you encounter inevitable bumps in the road. This chapter is all about prioritizing physical, emotional, and mental health to help you stay unstuck or regain lost ground moving forward.

What It Means to Prioritize Wellness

When you hear the term *wellness*, what pops into your mind? Images of social media influencers grinding it out at the gym or guzzling protein shakes instead of beers? Although regular exercise and making better nutritional choices are elements of healthy living, wellness involves a much broader context of behaviors and beliefs that promote the development of your best self.

The Global Wellness Institute defines *wellness* as "the active pursuit of activities, choices, and lifestyles that lead to a state of holistic health." Recognizing that wellness is often confused with terms such as *well-being*, *happiness*, and *health*, the institute clarifies that "while there are common elements among them, wellness is distinguished by not referring to a static state of being (i.e., being happy, in good health, or a state of well-being). Rather, wellness is associated with an active process of being aware and making choices that lead toward an outcome of optimal holistic health and well-being."[1] *Self-care*, a term I use often, is also related: it's the process of actively protecting your well-being, health, and happiness. This process is crucial when it comes to maintaining your current trajectory now that you're unstuck.

Why is prioritizing wellness so important? Living within your strongest, healthiest state of being creates more fulfillment and meaning. You are literally smarter, more capable, and more creative when you take care of yourself, rather than constantly pushing yourself without rest or maintenance. Consistent self-care enables you to look out for others, overcome obstacles, and bring more goodness into your life. It's a matter of making time for personal replenishment.

"We all want to deliver good work; take care of our family; and be the best mother, father, son, daughter we can be," said Brenda Bence, a global executive leadership coach and the author of *The Forgotten Choice: Shift Your Inner Mindset, Shape Your Outer World*. "But if your cup is empty, you'll have nothing left to pour into other people's cups. So you need to really pause and replenish; fill up your own cup so that you can offer more to others."

Your physical, mental, and emotional health are components of your well-being. You're probably familiar with how to take care of your physical body: eat a balanced diet, exercise regularly, and get enough sleep. Mental and emotional health are more neglected in our society but no less important; they require attention to other areas of your life that may not seem as concrete. *Greater Good* magazine, published by the Greater Good Science Center at UC Berkeley, has identified twelve building blocks of individual and community well-being—behaviors that research suggests will support your health and happiness and foster positive connections with other people.[2] The list includes:

- Altruism
- Awe
- Bridging differences
- Compassion
- Empathy
- Diversity
- Forgiveness
- Gratitude
- Happiness
- Mindfulness
- Purpose
- Social Connection

We've already covered many of these concepts throughout this book, such as self-compassion, knowing your purpose, practicing forgiveness, and gaining support through social connections. In the next few pages, you'll learn more about mindfulness, and then in chapter 13, we'll explore gratitude and altruism. The remaining building blocks are equally meaningful. Awe, the sense of wonder and amazement that you may feel when beholding natural treasures such as the Grand Canyon or the Northern

Lights, can improve your social well-being and make you more curious.[3] Bridging differences helps improve your understanding of others and builds more productive dialogue, while embracing diversity drives innovation. Empathy allows you to connect more deeply with other people. Happiness, which spans a spectrum of positive emotions ranging from contentment to overwhelming joy, can lead to greater life satisfaction.

All of these building blocks work together to enhance your wellness. Check out the individual quizzes that *Greater Good* offers under each topic on its website to note how you score.[4] Then use those results to determine areas where you'd like to improve, or a building block of strength you'd like to lean into deeper to gain as much goodness as possible. Select one of these concepts to practice. For example, you may want to add more awe-inspiring moments into your life. If nature prompts those feelings of wonderment, that might entail driving outside of the city limits to witness a meteor shower at night. If you feel the same way about classical music, it may mean attending an outdoor concert performed by a stellar symphony orchestra. Consider what makes your jaw drop with excitement and amazement, and plan to engage in that type of experience.

With any of these wellness building blocks, it's important to stay in the present moment to get the most out of it. When we spoke, Bence agreed, saying, "When you take care of yourself, whether through exercise, getting enough sleep, taking breaks and vacations, or mind rest, all of that shifts your energy into being in the present. You're not worrying about the past or dramatizing about the future. Being fully in your present helps you get unstuck and unlock your full potential because that is when we're most alive and capable of creating and thinking clearly."

The first step toward prioritizing wellness is becoming aware of what areas in your life need to be refueled before you completely run out of steam. Often, people tend to focus their attention on some areas while others drop by the wayside. For example, you may already prioritize altruism by volunteering at various community organizations, but if you're not careful, you'll get so caught up in those activities that your friendships (social connections) start to drop.

Notice, also, how your prime area of stuckness plays a role in these circumstances. For example, if you know that you're a Debbie Downer, you may need to spend more time on gratitude and empathy, and if you're not flexible, bridging differences can require deliberate thought and practice. Although it would be terrific to tick the box on every dimension of well-being, many of us don't have time for that. You may need to pick and choose wellness activities that yield the greatest bang for the buck in your world. A good starting point is to identify areas of personal wellness that need the most attention. (Check out the Take Action section for tips on accomplishing that step.) In the meantime, I've identified four areas that frequently fit this category—especially for people who are seeking to maintain their trajectory—and they are: exercise, nutrition, sleep, and mindfulness.

Regular movement does wonders for your well-being. The Mayo Clinic notes that exercise releases endorphins, which makes you feel better, helps reduce tension, and can increase your self-confidence.[5] Mental clarity also increases. The *American College of Sports Medicine* journal published an article about an experiment in which university students were asked to memorize a string of letters and then allowed to run, train with weights, or sit quietly. The students who ran were quicker and more accurate when tested than students who chose the other two options.

Unlike athletes, getting exercise probably isn't part of your job description, but maybe it should be. Ron Friedman, PhD, an award-winning psychologist and the author of *The Best Place to Work: The Art and Science of Creating an Extraordinary Workplace*, espouses that regular exercise is actually part of your job. "Instead of viewing exercise as something we do for ourselves—a personal indulgence that takes us away from our work—it's time we started considering physical activity as part of the work itself," he noted. "The alternative, which involves processing information more slowly, forgetting more often, and getting easily frustrated, makes us less effective at our jobs and harder to get along with for our colleagues."[6] I'd argue that the same is true for other areas of your life.

Healthy nutrition choices can also do wonders for wellness. A nine-year study of nearly three hundred Canadians, using data from the Canadian Community Health Survey, found that a higher fruit-and-vegetable intake was associated with lower odds of both depression and anxiety—even after controlling for age, gender, income, education, physical activity, chronic illness, and smoking.[7] And a 2013 study of 281 young adults found that their moods were better on days when they ate more fruits and vegetables. Fruit-and-vegetable consumption predicted positive moods for the next day as well.[8]

Although there's a plethora of information available on how to eat better, my advice is simple: pay attention to what you're eating each day and how you feel afterward. Often, patterns will start to emerge when you become more mindful of your eating habits. Perhaps you realize that popcorn doesn't agree with you, or that you feel sluggish after your afternoon soda. Or maybe you realize that you get hangry everyday around 4:00 p.m. Now you can choose one thing that you will change. For example, if you are "hangry" every day around this time, you may decide to add more protein to your midday meal or simply make an effort to always have a nutritious snack on hand. If you find this work difficult or don't know where to start, consider working with a nutritionist or health coach to determine which foods best support making your wellness a priority. We really *are* what we eat. Notice how certain foods impact your overall well-being, and plan meals accordingly. Every person is different, so understand what best supports you in thriving and staying unstuck for good.

Getting enough sleep seems like a no-brainer, but many of us simply do not prioritize this habit. According to the CDC, one in three adults do not get enough sleep (seven or more hours per day).[9] Yet it's vital for wellness. The U.S. Department of Health and Human Services notes that sleep improves your immune system, stress response, and mood; promotes clearer thinking and better interpersonal skills; allows people to stay at a healthy weight; and lowers the risk of developing serious health problems.[10] Research has also shown a proven link between effective leadership and sleep. Citing research reported in the *Occupational & Environmental*

Medicine Journal, Nick van Dam, McKinsey's global chief learning officer, and sleep expert Els van der Helm, wrote that moderate sleep deprivation, which they define as about seventeen to nineteen hours of wakefulness, is equal to that of a person with a blood-alcohol level of 0.05 percent, which is the legal drinking limit in many countries.[11] Yikes!

You see, the brain's prefrontal cortex directs what psychologists call executive functioning, including all the higher-order cognitive processes such as problem solving, reasoning, organizing, inhibition, planning, and executing plans. As the authors explain, although other brain areas can cope relatively well with too little sleep, the prefrontal cortex cannot. A good night's sleep is essential for effectively solving problems, seeking out different perspectives, increasing engagement, and supporting others—the very skills needed for effective leadership at work or in any part of our lives.

Last, let's get into *mindfulness*, a term that you may have heard of but not quite understood. The Mindful Awareness Research Center at UCLA defines mindfulness as "paying attention to present-moment experiences with openness, curiosity, and a willingness to be with what is." On the organization's website, it notes that "significant research has shown mindfulness to address health issues such as lower blood pressure and boost the immune system; increase attention and focus, including aid those suffering from ADHD; help with difficult mental states such as anxiety and depression, fostering well-being and less emotional reactivity; and thicken the brain in areas in charge of decision making, emotional flexibility, and empathy."[12] Even better, it's not hard to get started. Thinking about the activities you practiced to quiet your mind in chapter 3, remember that mindfulness starts by "being" instead of "doing." You can go for a walk and instead of listening to music, a podcast, or talking to a friend, focus on breathing and observing the world around you. Eating a meal mindfully means slowing down and savoring, rather than devouring, each bite, paying attention to the various aromas and tastes. Meditation has become an incredibly popular way to practice mindfulness, and you don't need to lock yourself in a dark room with a yoga mat to benefit from it. Numerous apps offer five-minute or shorter guided meditations for people at any level of experience, which will enhance your overall sense of well-being.

Even giving yourself one minute per hour to rest your mind can help. These mini mental breaks can help you relax and gain more clarity—and then allow you to return stronger to the task at hand. "I ask the executives I work with to take one minute—sixty seconds every hour—to sit back, relax, calm your mind, bring down your shoulders, and breathe deeply," explained Bence. "If you do that one minute for every waking hour, then you'll get about sixteen minutes or so a day of mental rest. That is just one example of how you can easily find time for taking care of yourself."

Anyone can make wellness a priority. Whatever shape you're currently in, whatever challenges you face, know that you can become more adept at building your capacity in this area. Practice and repetition are essential. Richard Davidson, PhD, a neuroscientist and the founder of the Center for Healthy Minds at the University of Wisconsin–Madison, agrees. "Well-being is a skill," he said. "All of the work that my colleagues and I have been doing leads inevitably to this central conclusion. Well-being is fundamentally no different than learning to play the cello. If one practices the skills of well-being, one will get better at it."[13]

If you're looking to make wellness a foundational behavior, I do have some strong advice about when to incorporate it into your schedule: become a morning person! Get up, say, an hour earlier, and take that "extra" time to focus on the areas of your wellness that need attention. Sure, you might be yawning just reading those words, feeling skeptical about breaking your habit of bingeing the latest streaming sensations until way past midnight. But even if you don't naturally rise before the crack of dawn, you can learn how to become one of those early birds that gets the worm. I certainly did. Back in 1992, I consciously decided to become a morning person and to exercise during that extra time. It was painful setting the alarm clock an hour earlier at first. But the burst of energy and self-esteem, and the way I felt after exercising, more than made up for it. I've continued this morning-exercise habit for more than thirty years now.

So what will *you* do with your extra hour? Perhaps you'll journal, practice yoga, meditate, or savor your morning coffee routine in order to get some peace and quiet before going to work.

Case Study: Meredith Moore

Self-care has been a lifeline for Meredith Moore—literally. Back in 2005, her life turned upside down. Six weeks after giving birth to her son, she was diagnosed with glioblastoma, the aggressive brain cancer that took the life of Senator John McCain. In the midst of experiencing three brain surgeries and a lifetime dose of radiation, Meredith lost her mother to breast cancer and her marriage unraveled. She went through a contentious divorce and surprised herself by falling in love with a close female friend.

"My life came to a screeching halt. I wondered if I would be alive a year from now," said Meredith. "I'd come to terms with being dealt a lot of trauma. But essentially, my metamorphosis was to become the person I am right now."

She also defied the odds. According to the Brain Tumor Charity, only 25 percent of glioblastoma patients survive more than one year, and 5 percent of patients last more than five years. Meredith, though, has been in remission for more than fifteen years. Embracing wellness has played a major role in keeping her healthy. She attributes much of her well-being today to building a detailed Morning Success Ritual.

Meredith starts each day by reading her quarterly game plan; and evaluating where she is in life, the people around her, her business, and other factors that matter the most. She asks herself powerful questions, visualizes success, evaluates goals, repeats positive affirmations (like a powerful mantra), and writes in her journal. Then she does physical exercise, paying attention to fatigue and respecting her limits. This detailed practice—supporting her physical, emotional, and mental wellness—continues to fuel a life that Meredith is grateful to live. She has grown personally and professionally because of these rituals. No matter how busy life becomes, she focuses on spending quality time with her wife, Kathy, and her now-teenage son. As the founder and CEO of the Artisan Financial Group, she has also become a nationally recognized financial expert who frequently speaks and writes about issues related to gender, money, and power.

Case Study: Suzanne Case

Making self-care a top priority helped Suzanne Case deal with one of the world's most stringent pandemic lockdowns. The global sports marketing expert moved to Sri Lanka on February 26, 2020, with a dream to start a surfing-and-fitness retreat. Having lived in Asia for years, the British ex-pat knew that the island paradise was the perfect place to incorporate her love of the sea, outdoors, fitness, and surf into a business. She found a place to live, started looking at land and properties, and relocated to Sri Lanka with the goal of making it her permanent home. Then two weeks later, the first local community-based case of COVID-19 was reported. Within another week, all international airports, schools, and parks were closed; work-from-home orders were declared; and island-wide curfews took effect to limit infections. But the intensive lockdown meant that no one was allowed to leave their homes for food, exercise, or any reason at all for three to seven days at a time. Even when the curfew was lifted, it was usually only four to fifteen hours at a time.

"I moved to Sri Lanka to start a new way of life, to regain an equilibrium, to pursue a dream, and to make my quality of life better," said Suzanne. "A month after I arrived, I find myself in a strange country, knowing few people and in total lockdown in a guesthouse thrown together with two virtual strangers—not knowing if I can stay in the country, where my next paycheck is coming from, and whether I can actually fulfill the reason I moved here."

Facing massive isolation and uncertainty about her career plans and tourist visa, Suzanne felt stuck. In order to cope, she focused intently on her well-being. Previously, she'd gone to the gym daily for weight-based training and only felt satisfied with intense workouts that left her exhausted. She'd already started adapting that approach to focus on a more balanced body-weight program. Switching to online instructors, classes that helped her relax, and other fitness tools, Suzanne took more time to focus on areas that she'd been neglecting, such as mobility and stretching. On non-lockdown days when she was permitted to leave her home, she would also take walks, swim in the sea, or relax outside.

Self-care also involved strengthening connections with key people. Suzanne scheduled daily check-ins with a good friend in the UK who was also starting her own business. She also had several video calls each week with her father and brother and got ongoing support from a virtual fitness community of like-minded souls. She learned a lot about herself during the lockdown. She removed self-imposed guilt about not being in constant motion and became more open about sharing her emotions. Before, it felt like the therapy she'd started ten years ago, motivated by a close family death, was a necessity. Now she views the counseling process as the best act of self-care she's ever undertaken and has been critical in helping her deal with isolation.

Suzanne also gained a greater belief in her self-reliance. She continued her more balanced approach to exercise and well-being after the lockdown ended and vaccines became available worldwide. "Pre-COVID-19, I rarely gave myself the time and space to slow down and look at the importance of self-care," she explained. "Most of the time I operated at breakneck speed, feeling unsuccessful unless I was constantly doing something. But being constantly busy is exhausting; it doesn't always produce the best outcome and doesn't allow me to always take care of myself. Now I know that self-care is vital to helping me actually achieve my dreams."

Take Action

Making wellness a priority can help you stay unstuck and allow you to bounce back quickly from any backsliding that may occur. The most effective way to start is to identify your greatest opportunities for improvement and strengthen those areas. Taking a number of measured steps will help you improve your resolve, capability, and commitment to wellness as a way of life.

Action 1: Identify which areas of personal wellness require the most attention. For the purpose of maintaining your trajectory, let's focus on the four concepts covered within this chapter. Be completely honest in assessing where you stand with each, and select the answer that best describes your current situation. Choose the area where you have the greatest deficit to concentrate on first. Once you get that down, come back to tackle the next area in need of improvement. I recommend starting small and going for manageable improvements—like going to bed fifteen minutes earlier each night for a week and then increasing it by another fifteen-minute increment the following week—in order to build a long-term habit.

Exercise—moving your body

1	2	3	4	5
I never make time for this	I do it occasionally, but it's not a priority	I do this sometimes	I do this regularly	It's a top priority for me

Nutrition—making healthy food choices

1	2	3	4	5
I never make time for this	I do it occasionally, but it's not a priority	I do this sometimes	I do this regularly	It's a top priority for me

Sleep—getting enough quality shut-eye

1	2	3	4	5
I never make time for this	I do it occasionally, but it's not a priority	I do this sometimes	I do this regularly	It's a top priority for me

Mindfulness—being in the present moment

1	2	3	4	5
I never make time for this	I do it occasionally, but it's not a priority	I do this sometimes	I do this regularly	It's a top priority for me

Action 2: Schedule your wellness. Analyze your calendar and choose a regular time when you can ensure that your wellness activity remains a top priority. Earlier, I recommended that you wake up one hour earlier and commit that hour to wellness. But if that doesn't work with your schedule, select a different time. It can even be your lunch hour, depending on your goals. For example, if the activity you choose is exercise, maybe go to a nearby gym for a spin class, where you'll have access to a quick shower. If you're trying to build a meditation habit, shut your door, pause all smart devices and electronics, and let yourself get recentered. If completely breaking away won't work for you, get creative and find healthy ways to multitask your desired activity. For Kathy Higgins, the chief executive officer of the nonprofit Alliance for a Healthier Generation, that means taking walking meetings. An avid fan of early-morning walks, Higgins often covers five to seven miles while catching up with team members during virtual, one-on-one meetings.

Action 3: Practice. Like any other skill, you'll get better at wellness when you practice it regularly. Whichever wellness behavior you choose to start with, commit to engaging in it at least three times a week. Once that becomes your normal routine, add additional days. Ideally, you'll build up to getting quality sleep, making healthy eating choices, exercising, and engaging in mindful behaviors most days of the week.

Action 4: Take mini mental breaks. As mentioned earlier, resting your mind for even one minute each hour can make a difference in your well-being. Set a regular timer on your smart device to remind yourself to do this several times throughout the day. Chances are good that a few days into this habit, you'll start looking forward to these energizing moments.

Action 5: Seek accountability. There are numerous ways to hold yourself accountable for your well-being. If you're the kind of person who likes consistent recognition in the form of badges and inspiring messages, check out apps that allow you to track desired behaviors and receive those electronic kudos in return—plus, you'll get to chart your progress. There are numerous free apps that provide this kind of accountability with sleep, nutrition, exercise, mindfulness, and more. You may also consider finding an accountability partner to share in this journey, someone like a friend or a partner who'd be delighted to check in with you daily on mutual accomplishments and challenges.

Action 6: Find fun ways to move your body. Make sure that the fitness activity you're looking to incorporate is fun instead of a chore; that will help you stick with it. Think about what you enjoy and how it could be incorporated in a different way that is more motivating. Perhaps you loved going out to nightclubs with your friends back in the day and now have figured out how to get your dance party on by taking Zumba classes. No matter what activity you're focusing on, give it a personal twist to bring fun into the equation.

Action 7: Develop a bedtime ritual. Getting better sleep is going to be on your list soon even if it's not the top priority at first. Make sure that you stop any screen time at least an hour before turning the lights out to create a consistent bedtime ritual that tells your body and mind that it's time to rest for the evening. That could mean creating a sleep sanctuary, which experts at Mii Amo Destination Spa in Sedona, Arizona, said involves keeping work out of the bedroom, setting your bedroom temperature cool for optimal sleep, adding fresh air whenever possible, sleeping in total darkness, and adding plants to naturally soak up toxins. You may also want to be mindful about beverage consumption, since REM (rapid eye movement) sleep is disrupted when there's alcohol in your system. Also, avoid after-dinner snacking to prevent heartburn.

Action 8: Create a food-mood journal. If you are trying to eat healthier, it can be helpful to recognize which situations prompt overeating or have you reaching for a bag of chips when you're in distress. Start by tracking what you ate and how you felt for several weeks. Notice which factors prompted undesirable actions, and also what happened and how you felt when doing really well. For example, you might find that eating cookies during an afternoon snack inevitably leads to an energy crash twenty minutes later, or you may see a pattern of feeling bloated and sleepy every time you eat pizza. Each person is different, so understand what best supports you in thriving and staying unstuck for good.

Exercise: 5 Things I Did for Myself Today

This is a really effective exercise. It reminds you to make wellness a top priority, and it involves noticing and increasing the amount of quality self-care actions you take each day.

All you have to do is (at night) reflect on the day. List any action or task you accomplished that was purely about your self-care. Don't include things you did to make another individual happy or something within the scope of your job or family responsibilities. This is just about you. The goal is to build up to five or more things each day that promoted your wellness and happiness.

At first, you may find it hard to come up with any actions. If this is the case, make a list of potential desired self-care behaviors that could be added to help you reach at least five. Getting enough sleep or a manicure would count, while dropping off the dry cleaning, a normal household chore, doesn't. Break things down into smaller tasks to keep you focused on accomplishing each goal. Let's use exercise as an example. When I do this exercise, I count the movement activity as one item and then stretching as a second one to get me more motivated to accomplish it.

As you're drifting off to sleep at night, recount all of the activities you accomplished to reinforce how wellness is a priority. Want extra credit? Record it in a quick journal entry, then plan what you'd like your five things list to include for the day ahead.

Notice how your list grows and, with it, the actions you're taking to prioritize wellness. Gamifying it in this manner can make you more determined to reach and exceed five items.

CHAPTER 12

Take Regular Internal Assessments

MAINTAINING YOUR POSITIVE MOMENTUM also involves paying attention to any emerging signs that things aren't going as well as desired. Regular maintenance is needed in order to stay unstuck, just as it would be for your car or home, so you can resolve an issue before a problem starts. After all, if you ignore a "check engine" light long enough, a breakdown is more than likely; it is inevitable.

As noted in the last chapter, life is going to get in the way, and challenges will test you despite your best intentions. The world doesn't stop rotating just because you were a Debbie Downer who learned how to choose optimism more frequently, or a formerly Shipwrecked individual who can ask for help now when needed. Taking regular assessments can help you stay on track, and live free and clear.

The truth is that it takes time to permanently change behaviors. Conventional wisdom used to dictate that twenty-one days were required to break a bad habit or build a new one. However, a study reported in the *European Journal of Social Psychology* in July 2009 indicated that, on average, it takes sixty-six days to build a new habit or change an existing one.[1] That amount of time can fluctuate depending on each person; researchers found that study participants successfully changed a particular behavior moving forward somewhere in the range between 18 and 254 days.[2]

"What we know now about people's brain scans and other information is that the average time for an individual to create a new habit is approximately two months," said hypnotherapist Inga Chamberlain, PhD, when I spoke to her about this topic. "But for some people, it will take up to a year because some habits are more deeply ingrained. Maybe they lack the desire to make that change. The repetition part will help it become more automatic, and for a person who's really excited about creating a new habit, the positive emotion will also make the mind absorb it more quickly."

Within this process of getting unstuck, you focused on changing not just one but numerous elements and practices to reach a better place. Recognizing that the first few months to a year of this new way of being could be the most vulnerable time for backsliding helps you be more aware of potential challenges. However, it could also happen down the road, when you inevitably face a situation that makes you more susceptible to derailment. External (and some internal) factors—such as a health crisis, a loss in the family, or some other stressor—will test you in the future, and these challenges can threaten to disrupt your path. Sometimes it's loud and obvious, while other times this appears quietly, like the slow reemergence of a bad habit or when the inner saboteur you worked so hard to quell suddenly works its way back in. That's when an early warning system is particularly helpful. This chapter shows you how to develop regular internal assessments to help gauge when things aren't as solid as you'd like, and need attention. Getting on top of those potential issues sooner rather than later allows you to nip problems and distractions in the bud and continue to thrive.

What It Means to Take Regular Internal Assessments

Taking regular internal assessments means checking in with yourself to determine if you're on track with your desired state. Ideally, you're taking a look inside consistently—say, every month—before anything goes too far sideways. This process of internal inquiry allows you to spot advance warning signs of behaviors or beliefs that need to be adjusted to keep you from backsliding. You're simply checking in to make sure that you're maintaining your chosen course.

The goal is not to punish or criticize yourself for reverting back to behaviors that may have contributed to your stuckness. Think of these assessments as a valuable defensive move, like checking the local weather forecast for word of impending storms that could impact a backyard cookout you've planned for the weekend. When you see that the likelihood of threatening skies is high, you may choose to move the social event indoors or reschedule it for another day—rather than be rained out at the last minute.

A number of common warning signs can signal that certain troubling issues are on the horizon. One of the biggest indicators is reverting back to what made you feel stuck before. Let's say that you were caught up in the pattern of You Don't Do You and learned how to embrace your authentic self. The relief you felt initially was tremendous; it was freeing to finally be true to yourself after spending so many years trying to conform to the expectations of others. Then, last week when you got together with a group of friends and everyone was sharing what kind of interesting vacations they were planning for the future, you talked about the prospect of cycling through Italy with your spouse . . . even though you can't afford a trip like that, and neither you nor your significant other would actually enjoy it. You only brought it up to fit in with what others were talking about.

Another warning sign is a general sense that things are off. After you got unstuck, your desired state of being might have been peace or a general sense of happiness. Now, it feels like you aren't quite in sync with that anymore. You might not be able to express exactly what's different yet, but something doesn't feel right. And your instincts or intuition—whatever you call it—is trying to alert you to find the root of the problem and fix it fast.

Your inner saboteur also gets louder when there's a potential for backsliding. The work you've done may have chilled out your inner saboteur to the point of being a vague whisper, if it bothers to show up at all. But recently, you've been hearing the insidious thoughts of that inner critic at a higher volume. That means some of the work you've done has gotten less solid.

Increased stress can also derail anyone. Operating at a high level of stress might be your norm, and you managed to get unstuck despite that. But things got worse, and now it feels like you're having a hard time keeping newly added positive behaviors intact. Pay attention to stress when it starts to elevate; it can throw you off your groove slowly at first, then hit you with a major unwelcome detour.

There are other warning signs that may be specific to you and your situation—lagging resolve, self-sabotaging behaviors, spikes of self-doubt, and more. When you see them start to bubble up, promptly explore the situation to ensure it doesn't harm your hard-won resolve. That's where proactive internal assessments come in. The most effective ones can be simple. At a minimum, you should be able to answer two important questions:

1. **Am I maintaining my desired state?** If the answer is "Yes," pat yourself on the back and celebrate. But if the answer is more like "I'm not sure," "Maybe," or a resounding "No," then it's time to dig in and correct your course. That's when you answer the second question.

2. **What will I do to get back on track ASAP?** (You'll see more practical tips about this point in the Take Action section.)

An internal assessment takes place as often as you feel it's needed. I recommend checking in with yourself more regularly during the first year of change—at least monthly—to quickly spot any immediate areas of concern. Some people flourish with more frequent bursts of looking inside, like journaling several times a week or having lunch with a trusted friend twice a month, where you serve as mutual accountability partners on these issues. Others prefer to have a quarterly check-in or even a more formal annual strategic pause. Hey, you've embraced authenticity and are living in alignment with your purpose as a normal behavior now. Think about what works best for you, and be sure that your check-in continues on the same maintenance schedule moving forward.

My favorite internal assessment tool is journaling. A journal is a safe place for you to reflect on your life, think about challenges and wins, work through issues, and gain perspective—important concepts to evaluate as part of your internal assessment process. If you're concerned about prying eyes trying to read it, consider using password-protected files or storing a physical journal in a safe, hard-to-find place.

Science has shown that journaling yields numerous benefits. According to the University of Rochester Medical Center in New York, journaling can help a person manage anxiety; reduce stress; cope with depression; prioritize problems, fears, and concerns; and offer a good opportunity for positive self-talk and identifying negative thoughts and behaviors.[3] Social psychologist and University of Texas at Austin professor James Pennebaker, PhD, found that journaling, which he refers to as "expressive writing," improves your emotional and physical well-being. He calls this process "life course correction," as writing about an issue that is causing anxiety can help you better deal with it.[4]

"Expressive writing gives us the opportunity to stand back and reevaluate issues in our lives," explained Pennebaker in an interview with Journaling.com. "One of the brain's functions is to help us understand events in our lives. Writing helps construct a narrative to contextualize trauma and organize ideas. Until we do this, the brain replays the same non-constructive thought patterns over and over and we become stuck. Writing about grief and trauma helps achieve closure, which tells the brain its work is done. This closure frees us to move forward."[5]

Being able to evaluate issues—and your thoughts and responses to them—is one of the most effective ways to determine if you're veering away from your desired state. Taking an internal assessment in this manner also allows you to identify triggers for stuckness that may not have been previously recognized. For example, a man I'll call Michael Simpson learned during an annual physical that he was at risk for becoming diabetic due to poor dietary choices that caused an unhealthy weight gain. Simpson realized that his habit of eating sugary treats several times a day contributed to concerning blood work and extra pounds. He built that habit in childhood, when his mother used to bake cookies and brownies daily for the family as a way to show affection. Simpson decided to cut back on refined sugar with the help of a nutrition coach. His blood work significantly improved, he lost the extra pounds, his energy level increased, and he felt a lot better overall.

During the next six months, he was pummeled by a series of challenges—his life partner became unemployed, and a burst water pipe demolished their home—but Simpson kept his healthy habits going. Things got better, and then Halloween, his favorite childhood holiday, rolled around. Simpson kept anxiously looking at the candy they handed out to neighborhood kids but didn't partake—until the next day at work. Simpson got into a mild disagreement with a coworker, and it became the proverbial straw that broke the camel's back. He dug into the Halloween candy that coworkers had brought into the office, eating massive handfuls of fun-sized goodies in a desperate attempt to feel better. It backfired. Within thirty minutes he felt terrible, sluggish, unable to concentrate, and angry at himself. What became clearer later, as Simpson journaled to figure out what had happened, was that he was exhausted from sustained months of stress. He always associated sugary treats with comfort, and turned to the candy because he needed a break, not a sugar crash that made him feel worse. With the insight from that internal assessment, Simpson was better able to anticipate and handle future challenges to his desired wellness.

Are you wondering how often you should use journaling to assess your current frame of mind? I'd say whenever the mood strikes you. When I have a lot going on, journaling several times a week helps me stay grounded and maintain a more balanced perspective. Pennebaker recommends that you journal for at least three to four days in a row to get a handle on what's affecting your life or worrying you, focusing on your deepest emotions and thoughts.[6] Some people can quickly blurt out everything on a computer file, smart device, or notepad, while others prefer to take their time to carefully ponder current circumstances. When you determine what works best, journaling can be a powerful tool in helping you stay on track and thrive.

Barbara Fagan-Smith, the chief catalyst for Living ROI and the author of *Living ROI: A Weekly Guide for Soulful Living*, concurs. "I think reflecting back and looking forward has been one of the most powerful things I've done," she said during our discussion. "That wasn't part of my practice for most of my journaling years, where I used to check in about how I felt or what was happening in my life. Now I'm seeing if my life reflects the priorities I've defined as most important to me, like family connection and personal wellness."

Fagan-Smith started journaling as a preteen more than forty years ago. This lifelong practice has allowed her to think through challenges and maintain a healthy perspective throughout different phases of life. When she worked as a London-based television producer for ABC News, covering revolutions in Eastern Europe and the 1990–1991 Gulf War, journaling helped Fagan-Smith deal with the constant threat of violence and death. It became a grounding resource as she got married and raised two now-adult children in the San Francisco Bay area. Journaling also helped her stay focused on building ROI Communication, which is the largest independent consulting firm focused exclusively on employee communication and engagement; create her encore career helping others with Living ROI; and deal with stressors like the

COVID-19 pandemic, illnesses, and natural disasters. (You'll learn more about how to build a journaling habit to conduct internal check-ins at the end of this chapter.)

An important element of taking regular internal assessments involves maintaining healthy personal boundaries. When you focus too much on the needs, requests, and desires of others, it can interfere with the process of listening intently to yourself to ensure you maintain your desired trajectory. Saying no to others can often make the difference in saying yes to yourself more often. Chad A. Buck, PhD, of Vanderbilt University explained that an effective personal boundary "is neither too rigid nor too loose. It offers protection while still keeping you connected to others, it offers structure, it limits the energy you devote to a person or situation, and it offers you choices rather than obligations or expectations. Visualize a stone wall with a gate that can be opened or closed. You are the gatekeeper, and no one gets access unless you say so."[7]

Consider what kind of boundaries you should create or keep in place to stay unstuck. Perhaps you limit phone calls to a parent who's always critical, or avoid spending time with a particular social group that seemed to bring out the worst in you. Boundaries are important even when fully engaged with the wonderful support system you built in chapter 10. You need to feed yourself first, and I mean that in terms of energy and time, before giving back to others.

Case Study: Ali Davies

When it comes to internal assessments, Ali Davies is a big believer. Evaluating her life in that manner and finding it lacking prompted a major shift more than twenty years ago, and regular check-ins have been the key to her continued success and evolution. Growing up as a Gen Xer in England, Ali thought that the normal progression of life

included education; a career; and then obtaining the house, spouse, and kids. She climbed the ladder at two global beverage companies by her early thirties and got married. But she felt unfulfilled.

"I started to wonder, if I was so successful, why I was feeling miserable?" said Ali. "Instead of the bottom line, I was more focused on people. It made me realize that the definition of success I was chasing wasn't what for me would constitute a successful life."

A tipping point came on January 1, 2000, when she and her husband, Martin, ditched a local New Year's Eve party to continue a deep conversation at home about their mutual dissatisfaction with their corporate careers. They woke up early the next morning to continue that talk while hiking up their favorite mountain, Jacob's Ladder in Derbyshire, England. "As we got to the top of this mountain, literally dawn was just breaking," she noted. "It was one of the most spiritual moments I've ever had watching the sun come up on this new millennium. We made the decision to find a different way to live and work that reflects our values."

From that initial place of deeply checking in with themselves, they spent the next few years actively designing the life they wanted, saving money, and making changes. Martin went back to college to become a physiotherapist, and Ali became a change consultant and coach. They moved to Ireland with their young son and enjoyed a more outdoorsy, relaxed pace of life. Regular check-ins, at least annually, allowed them to stay on course. After a few years, Martin was involved in a very serious car crash that nearly killed him. During a camping trip several months into his recuperation, the two realized that it was time to pursue their ultimate dream of living in Canada.

In 2013, Ali and Martin relocated to the Vancouver area. Now Canadian citizens, it is their forever place. Ali flexed her career to spend more time with her son, and with his impending departure for college, she's now upping her professional game. In addition to her Change in Action coaching business, she's the founder of Outside of the Circle, a global community dedicated to helping high-level professionals redefine success to design their next chapter in life.

Over the past two decades, Ali has given herself an internal assessment once a year to ensure that she continues to live by her values. It reinforces what is going well and helps determine if further change is necessary. Her process starts by choosing the right location to optimize creative thinking. Recognizing that she does her best thinking outdoors in nature, Ali conducts her internal assessment in August when it's warm outside, most often while sitting in a chair on a beach surrounded by notebooks to record her thoughts. Step 1 of her internal assessment process involves reviewing her definition of success to determine if it's still on point or needs to evolve, and then reviewing values and what matters most to her personally and professionally. Armed with her current or revised definition of success, Ali then reviews and updates her vision of what her ideal state is in life, a playful process that can involve daydreaming.

Her next step involves making that vision a reality, determining what she needs to concentrate on for the next 12 months. At this point, Ali creates action plans and commitments, and figures out her execution steps for the year ahead. Then she answers a series of self-assessment questions to gain clarity on her behaviors, habits, mindset, emotional state, support needed, and more. "People usually heavily lean to focusing on what we needed to do," explained Ali. "That is important, but equally important and often overlooked is who we need to BE." She then concludes the process by placing a structure and framework in place to keep her on tracking moving forward.

"People believe logistics is the hardest part about making a shift, and what stops them. But the biggest obstacles are actually emotions, beliefs, their mindset, and change agility," she added. "Rather than being prompted by a setback, internal assessments should be a natural part of life."

Take Action

The purpose of an internal assessment is to identify and plan the maintenance steps you need to get back on track with your journey of staying unstuck. Follow these steps to get the most out of that process:

Action 1: Be consistent. Determine how often you wish to conduct internal assessments, and then stick to that schedule. Being consistent will allow you to compare previous check-ins and see if your confidence level or positive habits are wavering at all. You may opt for monthly internal assessments during the first year and then move to doing that twice a year afterward.

Action 2: Use numerical assessments. Numerical measurements are a great way to track your continued progress and maintenance. Focus on the area in which you got unstuck—let's use building self-trust and confidence as an example. Refer back to the desired state you described in chapter 3; perhaps for you it's "the absence of self-doubt." List the behaviors, actions, and beliefs you changed in order to get unstuck and achieve that state. With this example, the factors you changed may have been regularly focused on what you like rather than dislike about yourself, replacing negative self-talk with positive affirmations, and forgiving yourself for making a mistake years ago that continued to plague your confidence.

Now, rate each factor on a scale of 1 (worst) to 10 (best) with respect to how well you're sticking to it. Whenever that number is a 7 or less, it's time to reinforce the process with the steps you used to get unstuck. So if the first two are coming in at an 8, but backtracking in self-forgiveness has slipped to a 4, that's what you should concentrate on strengthening once more. You can also check in using the Wheel of Life (an exercise from chapter 4) once or twice a year to determine which areas of your world need more reinforcement and support.

Action 3: Journal your assessment. If you prefer to engage in expressive writing, I recommend that you answer these basic questions to establish a baseline that can be used as a point of comparison moving forward: *Am I maintaining my desired state? Why is this the case? What will I do to get back on track? What have I learned about myself as a result of this process?*

Action 4: Get input. Ask trusted resources—the friends and professionals who have really been there for you in your network of support, how you're doing. Their honest responses can awaken you to issues or progress that you may not have noticed yourself. This can be done face-to-face or during a video session or a phone call, or you can email these individuals so they can answer that question if you feel that they'll be able to be more open if you're not engaging in person.

Action 5: Identify your warning signs. In chapter 11, I discussed some general warning signs to help you spot when things are slightly off or have the capacity to become a future issue. Now, list the warning signs that are specific to you and your situation, choosing somewhere between three to six that will help you quickly determine when reinforcement is needed.

Let's say that your area of stuckness involved being on a road to nowhere. You identified your purpose and motivation in this process of getting unstuck and feel great about that. However, is there a worst-case scenario that triggers a sense of being lost or off-course, like auditioning for multiple acting roles and not making the cut, or pitching a business idea to potential investors and coming up short? Brainstorm about situations and people that could be triggers for backsliding behavior in order to reinforce and strengthen your new way of being before facing a significant challenge.

Action 6: Acknowledge your progress. Internal check-ins are not just about identifying areas of concern. Recognize what you're doing well, and celebrate your continued growth. Think about progress charts or report cards that feature stickers, badges, and happy emojis. How can you recognize and applaud your continuation on the desired path you identified in chapter 3?

Action 7: Make your recovery plan. When you see yourself slipping in terms of living in alignment with your purpose, it's time to come back to the light with an active recovery plan. The first step is to revisit your desired state and statement of purpose to be completely clear about your goals. Reflect on why you backtracked, and list three to five actions that you plan to take to return to your positive trajectory. Reinforce those actions by revisiting whichever exercises within this process were most helpful in addressing your particular kind of stuckness. It might be time to craft a new vision board (see chapter 3) or practice an inward trust fall (see chapter 5) to remind yourself how good it feels to be living life on your own terms. Identify how you'll know that you're back to your desired state, and then check in with yourself at least monthly moving forward in order to monitor your progress.

Action 8: Plan an annual strategic pause. As you may do with a recovery plan, use the tools from chapter 3 that helped you identify your desired state, and the purpose statement you crafted at the end of chapter 4. Follow the instructions in that section to honor the pause, remove distractions, reflect on your purpose, set an intention, and plan the logistics accordingly. Refer to your personal list of warning signs to see if there are any early indicators of potential challenges that need to be addressed.

Exercise: Build a Journaling Habit

I'm a big believer in using journaling to conduct internal assessments and promote your overall well-being. Just remember to be patient as you put this tool into practice. Journaling starts with being more intentional in terms of listening to and loving yourself. Don't expect change overnight. My biggest "aha" moments usually come after weeks of writing regularly about a few items; and then suddenly, the truth, answer, or solution I'm seeking can hit me like a bolt of lightning. Inevitably it is followed by more weeks or longer of practice before the next nugget hits. Here are the steps:

1. Plan how to use this practice for check-ins. Will you answer a couple of simple assessment questions or go more into depth? Is comparing metrics part of this process? Determine how often you plan to execute this process.

2. Choose your medium. When I first started journaling as a therapeutic tool about thirty years ago, I wrote my thoughts out by hand into lovely hand-bound books. Over the years, I found that my writing speed simply couldn't keep up with all of the insights running through my brain at once. I shifted to using a computer, which allowed me to quickly download thoughts with a keyboard. Now, most days I open a new Word document on my laptop and let it fly. Other people prefer writing their thoughts into a specially designated book, typing notes into their smartphone, or using a voice-recording app to speak their truth and get insight by playing it back. The most effective medium for you is going to be the one that you'll actually use.

3. Ditch any pressure. Are you waiting to sound like William Shakespeare when recording your deepest thoughts? That kind of self-induced pressure can be paralyzing, which defeats the purpose of letting everything come out to put things into context. I recommend starting the internal assessment process by identifying if you're on track, and if not, what you plan to do to correct that.

4. Write in a stream-of-consciousness format for at least ten to fifteen minutes. This is where you just write, type, or say whatever pops into your mind without caring about punctuation, using highfalutin vocabulary words, and the like. Write as long as you like; your only limit is the time you've allocated to this activity. Remember that this is for your eyes only, not anyone else's ... if you have no desire to share.

5. Seek accountability partners. You don't have to share what's written in your journal with anyone else, but some people benefit from doing this process with those they trust. Fagan-Smith engages in a weekly journaling process every Sunday with two friends, which creates more support and accountability for her journaling process. All three of them are entrepreneurs whose children are about the same age, creating multiple commonalities. Knowing that someone is holding you accountable for dealing with an issue or changing a behavior can create a greater sense of urgency in dealing with that situation. Keep in mind that your accountability partners can shift at different times in your life. A close friend might not be the right person, though others who are focusing on similar business or personal goals can provide the support you need. The key is finding someone who is also committed to having an intentional life. Choosing multiple people ensures that even if one person is unavailable, the weekly sessions can continue with some participants from your small group.

6. Recognize your wins. You don't want a journal to be a place that you only visit during hard times. Note what you're doing well, and pause to let yourself celebrate those victories. This is true during an internal assessment or at any point when you wish to stay in touch with yourself.

7. Revisit earlier entries. Going back to previous journal entries is the best way to measure your growth and progress. Earlier in the book, I referenced my quarter-life crisis at age twenty-five, which was fully recorded in handwritten journal entries. I visited that original journal for years to remember what that sense of despair felt like and cheer myself on for working hard to get unstuck and move past it.

CHAPTER 13

Practice Gratitude

THE FINAL STEP in remaining on your desired path involves practicing gratitude. Although we've touched on being grateful in other chapters, gratitude is such a powerful tool in maintaining your trajectory that it deserves center stage here. Think of gratitude as the whipped cream and cherry topping off an already delicious ice cream sundae. You've completed all the work in this process to get unstuck and now have a deeper, more meaningful relationship with yourself. Your hard-won desired state has been reinforced as you prioritize wellness and take regular check-ins with yourself to stay on track. Now gratitude, which has been scientifically proven to enhance every part of your life, locks it all in and strengthens your resolve.

Our journey to this point really has been about *you*—empowering you to break free and unleash your full potential. Hopefully you're feeling grateful and proud of yourself for putting in the work to have a better life. And from that place of gratitude, consider how you can contribute to the world—because you now have the tools to amplify your purpose and reinforce your unstuckness by focusing on more than just yourself.

In this chapter, you'll learn more about the transformative power of gratitude, how to leverage it as "rocket fuel" for your personal journey, and how to adopt fulfilling gratitude practices in your daily life. We'll also explore a sometimes overlooked way to practice gratitude: giving back to others, which can help you find perspective and positively reinforce your actions while improving the lives of those in your world.

What It Means to Practice Gratitude

Gratitude is a positive state of mind in which you lead with appreciation. It's a feeling of being thankful for things big and small—a sunny day after a week of rain, finding lasting love, your new job, or scoring an amazing deal on those jeans you've been stalking online. It doesn't have to be about tangible things either; you can feel gratitude about spiritual beliefs, receiving support from a higher power, and more.

Studies have demonstrated numerous links between gratitude and improved health and wellness. One of the world's leading experts on the science of gratitude, psychology professor Robert Emmons, PhD, of the University of California, Davis, found in one study that gratitude led to 23 percent lower levels of stress hormones (cortisol), a 10 percent improvement in sleep quality in patients with chronic pain, and a 7 percent reduction in biomarkers of inflammation in patients with congestive heart failure.[1] His research also concluded that activities such as keeping a gratitude journal or writing letters of thanks helped people reduce dietary fat intake by as much as 25 percent and reduced the risk of depression in at-risk patients by 41 percent over a six-month period.[2] Gratitude research conducted at the University of Southern California (USC) reinforced how gratitude positively impacted health, social bonding, and stress relief. The study showed how gratitude impacts brain structures, finding positive implications tied to social bonding, reward, and other benefits.[3]

Other research has shown that gratitude improves self-esteem and mental health, promotes resilience, increases empathy, and strengthens mental fortitude.[4] In fact, being grateful can help people better cope with trauma. A 2006 study published in *Behaviour Research and Therapy* found that Vietnam War veterans with higher levels of gratitude experienced lower rates of post-traumatic stress disorder.[5]

What's more is that actively expressing your gratitude to yourself and others on a regular basis increases its resonance, removing any limits on what is possible in living in alignment with your purpose. According to neuroscientist Glenn Fox, an expert in the science of gratitude at the USC Marshall School of Business, "The limits to gratitude's health benefits are really in how much you pay attention to feeling and practicing gratitude."[6]

There are several fulfilling ways to express gratitude in your daily life. Consider keeping a basic gratitude journal (which is different from the more in-depth journaling exercise explored in chapter 12 for conducting an internal assessment) by jotting down notes whenever you feel a surge of thanks. According to a 2015 study conducted by the American Psychological Association, patients who kept gratitude journals for eight weeks showed reductions in levels of several inflammatory biomarkers while they wrote.[7] The Gratitude Rocket Fuel exercise at the end of this chapter is a great tool for focusing on everything and everyone that fills your heart with gratitude and leveraging that positive sense to create more meaning and momentum.

Gratitude increases when you thank others; research has shown that expressing thanks benefits the recipient of your gratitude as well as your own well-being. That's because you make people feel seen, increasing their motivation. A study conducted by the Wharton School of the University of Pennsylvania found that employees who were thanked by grateful leaders made 50 percent more fundraising calls than their peers who weren't recognized in that same manner.[8] Acknowledging others in this manner improves your relationship with them.[9] Even expressing a quick thanks to people you don't know well or at all can make a difference. A 2014 study published in *Emotion* found that thanking new acquaintances for helping you with a project or making a contribution in some way makes them more likely to seek an ongoing relationship.[10]

Noticing what makes you grateful increases that positive feeling. Remember the reticular activating system (mentioned in chapter 2), the part of your brain that brings whatever you're focusing on, positive or negative, to the forefront of your awareness? Focusing on what makes you grateful each day creates more gratitude, which brings even more positive developments into your life.

There's also another way to practice gratitude that you may not have considered: giving back. Assisting people in need helps you gain a broader perspective on society and your own life. Witnessing the significant challenges faced by others can illustrate how fortunate you are, increase your gratitude, and foster a desire to be of service.

Anda Goseco, ICF-PCC, a global executive coach based in the Philippines, told me that it's a matter of perception. "When you reach out to others, it puts things in perspective," she noted. "You get to see that your problem is not as big as you thought it would be or recognize all the similarities you have with the situations of others. That connection of helping people brings out the human side of you. When you give, you're helping others and yourself, as it reinforces your capacity and internal strength," continued Goseco. "It creates a feeling also of oneness, that you're not alone."

Curious about how to start giving back? Don't feel like you have to support a cause out of expectation or peer pressure. It can be tempting to say yes to every opportunity to help. However, overcommitting yourself can hinder your well-being. Sure, I've been involved with numerous causes on a project basis, particularly in my corporate roles where overseeing social responsibility is part of the job description. But my giving groove—what feels best and because of that, is a joy, not a chore—has been acts of mentorship, and I've given advice to hundreds of people along the way in that manner.

I recommend that you determine how you want to be of service and the best parameters for bringing that to life. Let's say you sign up for a weekend slot helping your company build a Habitat for Humanity house. That's fantastic. However, it doesn't mean that you should feel obliged to volunteer during every day off until the project is complete. Saying no or delaying a nonurgent request for help to honor plans with family or friends is healthy and in your best interests.

Genuine altruism, stemming from a deep desire to help people and the community, is good for you. Volunteering your time and participating in acts of kindness bolsters your mental health;[11] feeling more socially connected prevents loneliness and depression. It can also improve your physical well-being. A 2013 study out of Carnegie Mellon University published in *Psychology and Aging* found that adults over age fifty who volunteered on a regular basis were less likely to develop high blood pressure, which contributes to conditions such as heart disease and strokes, than nonvolunteers.[12]

There's a lot to be said for being thankful. In the United States there's an entire holiday devoted to it: Thanksgiving. This has always been my favorite holiday, completely aside from the story of pilgrims and their ultimately fraught relationship with the Native Americans who occupied the country first. I love bringing friends and family together to eat turkey, pumpkin pie, and British dishes such as duck fat potatoes and Yorkshire pudding that my expat hubby has introduced to our feast. My favorite part of all is when we all go around the table and acknowledge what we're thankful for. For me, hearing people reflect in gratitude about overcoming challenges and accomplishing certain milestones fills my heart with joy. At this point, those tidbits are even tastier than sweet-potato casserole.

Case Study: Abby Maxman

Choosing to respond to a health crisis with gratitude has helped Abby Maxman thrive. From the moment she joined the Peace Corps in Southern Africa after graduating college, Abby has focused on making the world a better place—literally. She and her husband joined the humanitarian organization CARE in entry-level roles, providing on-the-ground assistance during the Rwandan genocide. They lived in Ethiopia; Haiti; parts of the former Soviet Union including Georgia, Armenia, and

Azerbaijan; and the Middle East, helping people facing devastating circumstances.

Then personal adversity struck in 2003, when they lived in Tbilisi, Georgia. A new mother, Abby was busy raising their young son and juggling numerous work commitments. When she found a lump in her groin, it was easy to dismiss. "Despite having cancer in our family and in our life, there was the feeling that there's no room for it to be something," she explained. "There's no time. I'm a mom. I'm breastfeeding, working, doing work I care deeply about."

Local doctors misdiagnosed it as a minor issue. When Abby came back to the United States for what she thought was going to be minor surgery, it turned out to be non-Hodgkin's Lymphoma. "I remember very viscerally when I was diagnosed, and fear set in," noted Abby, who ended up undergoing two years of chemotherapy, radiation, and surgery. "Different scenarios set in, and I felt stuck. I wanted to survive this battle and decide how I chose emotionally and physically to muscle my way through things or not."

Gratitude helped Abby move forward. "I felt nothing but gratitude for having access to the world's best health care," she said. "That gave me the confidence to get through things." She felt incredibly grateful for her husband and son, family, friends, and having a supportive workplace. She kept a mental "hope chest" of positive thoughts and her dreams for the future, such as having more children, as she finished one phase and got to the next one. She continued working with those less fortunate, which helped her maintain a grateful perspective. Before surgery, Abby froze her eggs with the determination to expand their family through birth or adoption—an act of hope.

Abby's treatment was a success, and she entered remission. Several years later, she started IVF and became pregnant with twins. Today, she serves as the president and CEO at Oxfam America and lives in the Boston area with her family. And, gratitude continues to be a driving force in her life. "Today, my gratitude has never been larger or deeper—for my beloved husband and three children, loved ones and friends, for my health, and for the privilege of serving and leading Oxfam America, where I can continue to contribute to our vision of a just world without poverty," said Abby. "I feel fortunate in so many ways."

Case Study: Spencer Koeneman

When Spencer Koeneman was twelve years old, his parents sent him to a church summer camp at Win Our World Urban Ministry in Knoxville, Tennessee. That weeklong experience volunteering to help the homeless proved to be transformative. He recounts an afternoon distributing cups of water to homeless people congregating on a local bridge in the middle of summer. "It was sweltering," said Spencer. "Everyone thanked us, and it made me realize that if a cup of water means that much to someone, what else can I do? It's humbling and a good way to put things in perspective."

Spencer asked the organizers if he could do more. Soon he started spending three weeks at the camp each summer, eventually leading groups of teens volunteering at homeless shelters and other nonprofit organizations. That desire to help others flourished. An avid fencer who traveled nationwide to tournaments, Spencer began providing complimentary lessons to kids who couldn't afford it while mentoring them to learn skills like CPR. The recent college graduate also volunteered as a referee at the Special Olympics while attending the University of South Carolina.

Helping others has helped Spencer grow in many ways. It broadened his perspective about people and the world overall, and he became more patient and open-minded. "I grew up in an upper-middle-class household and never had to worry about financial issues," he explained. "To volunteer at a transitional housing shelter and have a resident thank a bunch of teens for helping him have a place to live for another month is so impactful. You gain the perspective of what it's like for other people.

I realized that you never know what's going on in the background, and sometimes people get dealt a bad hand."

Giving back has also helped Spencer realize the value of trusting his instincts and not relying on immediate gratification. "When you're volunteering, there isn't that much instant feedback," he added. "You just have to accept that what you've done has helped without ever seeing its impact. You've done the best that you can, and you have to move on."

Take Action

Practicing gratitude reinforces all of the great work you've done to get unstuck and stay that way. Here are some actions you can take to increase your level of appreciation and thankfulness overall:

> **Action 1: Identify the people you appreciate.** Think about the individuals in your life you're grateful for, and list them, along with a brief reason why. It could be your aunt for encouraging you to attend college when no one else believed you could do it, a coworker who covered for you on a holiday so you could spend time with your kids, or a neighbor who takes in your mail and packages when you're out of town. Make that initial list and then update it on a monthly basis.
>
> **Action 2: Express thanks.** Focusing on one or two people a week from the list you created, start thanking each person for the positive impact they've made on you. Do this by email, phone, text, or an old-fashioned letter; the method doesn't matter as much as the act of reaching out in acknowledgment and thanks. Be specific about something they did or said, or describe a behavior they displayed that had a lasting effect on you. For example, I wrote a letter to my high school AP English teacher, Karen Kaminsky, about five years after graduation when

I was working in my first corporate communications job. When I looked back at my education, I realized that she was the best teacher I'd ever had and wanted her to know that. I mailed the letter, and a few weeks later, she wrote me a note back about what that meant to her. Decades later, the feeling of that action still makes me smile.

Action 3: Practice acts of kindness. Aim to practice at least one act of kindness each week. Being there for others doesn't mean that you have to dramatically change your lifestyle or habits. You don't have to go big or go home; reaching out with small acts of kindness can make a noticeable impact—for example, picking up groceries or bringing in a trash can from the curb for a neighbor who lacks mobility; spending an hour tutoring a child who needs help; donating blood to the Red Cross; or teaching coworkers how to upgrade their presentation skills, bolstering their confidence and job performance in the process. When my father died in 2001, I came back from the funeral to find that some of my close friends had cleaned my apartment, restocked the fridge, and even changed the sheets on my bed. That burst of loving support helped me when I needed it most.

Action 4: Give back to a meaningful cause. Are you ready to become more involved in volunteer work, either on a onetime basis here and there or as an ongoing commitment? Selecting an organization near and dear to your heart makes that experience more meaningful. I know people who have pursued acts of service to bolster their college applications or who've joined a nonprofit board to advance their careers and business networking possibilities. There's nothing wrong with that, as you're still putting good out into the world. But if you're going to invest your time and passion in something on a continual basis, focusing on a cause that resonates with you deeply is more likely to lift your spirits and promote a strong sense of accomplishment.

Exercise: Gratitude Rocket Fuel

Gratitude just might be the ultimate sustainable substance. After all, it's easy to create on demand and has a low carbon footprint. I believe that getting a daily, deliberate dose of gratitude can act like rocket fuel in reinforcing your efforts to get unstuck, master self-doubt, and fulfill your amazing potential in life. That's why I created this exercise to stoke your gratitude supply each day and help maintain your current trajectory.

Begin your morning with this tool to frame the day ahead, or do it before bedtime to reflect on what you've accomplished. Best of all, you can see results from investing as little as ten to fifteen minutes of time. Here are the six steps to take:

1. Create. Open a new Word document on your laptop, the notes screen on your phone, or go old school and take out a blank piece of paper and pen. Take in a deep breath and then exhale. Stop paying attention to whatever else is around you, and focus intently on the page in front of you. Back away from your technology. Ignore the beeps and buzzes that notify you about likes and connection requests. Make sure your devices are on airplane mode, or even better, nowhere near you.

2. Consider. Answer a few questions to get a good understanding about your current circumstances, starting with: "How do I feel today, and why?" Keep the answer simple: "I feel rested and happy from getting enough sleep, ready to tackle the day," or "I'm frustrated because I overate from stress and didn't take good care of myself." Expand on that line of thought a bit by focusing on the why behind it. Then ask: "What else am I thinking about?" Include any other "aha" moments or clarifying thoughts that pop into your mind.

3. Acknowledge. Think about what you did for yourself during the previous day, or in the case of a nighttime practice, the day you just completed. This step is about expressing gratitude to yourself. It acts as proof of the depth of your commitment. List whatever comes to your mind, making sure you note at least one item. This could be that you got enough sleep, walked your dog, exercised, didn't break out the potato chips when work got stressful, found twenty minutes to enjoy an inspiring podcast, and so on. It doesn't have to be particularly ambitious. When I first started this exercise, "taking a minute to think about my life" made the list before evolving into a full daily practice.

4. List. Make a list of everything you're grateful for at that moment, and the longer the better. Ever since I started doing this exercise, my daily list has skyrocketed from four or five items to well over twenty. It doesn't matter if some items are slightly repetitious. For example, my list from a few months ago included: good health, walked with a friend, the blue dress in my closet that became tight fits better now, finished writing an article, my loving husband, had a good Zoom call with my eighty-three-year-old mom, and more. I usually start by listing things related directly to me (good health, ability to exercise, making progress on my book), and then move on to the people and relationships I'm grateful for before adding other things. And you don't necessarily have to be meaningful and profound. I bought a car back in December 2017 that I really like. I named her Simone during the test drive because in my mind she has the dramatic personality of a French soap-opera actress. So Simone made my daily gratitude list for a while, too.

5. Leverage. Review your gratitude list, savoring what you're grateful for and acknowledging your role in creating these circumstances or receiving positive developments. Then leverage that sense of positive well-being to ask for more. Note up to three to five new items that you want to claim, based on the belief that it is possible. You could list "Drink ten glasses of water a day," or "Save money to buy a road bike"—the point is that the gratitude you've been feeling is now harnessed as rocket fuel to create more goodness.

6. Reinforce. This exercise is living proof of your ability to maintain your trajectory. It shows how you've gotten unstuck in the past, how you can now ask for more, and is a great reinforcement of your capacity to easily bounce back from any backslides or derailments that may lie ahead. I can't stress enough that acknowledging your victories is key. Those small wins will help strengthen your resolve, correct your course as needed, and lead to successful long-term maintenance of your desire state.

Motivational speaker Brian Tracy once said, "Develop an attitude of gratitude, and give thanks for everything that happens to you, knowing that every step forward is a step toward achieving something bigger and better than your current situation." I couldn't agree more.

Gratitude is a powerful source of energy. Harnessing it with this practice will help you thrive and get back on track as needed.

CONCLUSION

WOW. HERE YOU ARE, at the end of this book. When we first started this journey, you were feeling chronically stuck in some way—it might have been in *multiple* ways. But you were willing to put in the work. As you've reevaluated your life goals and considered making major changes, I hope that *Free and Clear: Get Unstuck and Live the Life You Want* has given you an effective road map and so much more when it comes to living in alignment with your purpose and goals—and that your lifestyle today is infused with greater fulfillment and meaning. Personally and professionally, you are crushing it in every sense of the word!

I'd like to leave you with a few parting thoughts, sort of like the party favors or goodie bags you'd take home after attending a swanky special event.

You are in charge of your life. Whatever relationships, obligations, or ties you have with others, you are ultimately in the driver's seat of your destiny. Sure, you might have put your dreams on hold for a while and for good reason. But now, it's *your* time to shine; so kudos to you for reaching for a better, happier existence.

All of the changes you've made working through the *Free and Clear* process—the goodness you've brought into your life—is due to you. I wrote this book to serve as an ultimate guide in helping you get unstuck in any area of life. But *you* are the one who worked through it—the one who showed up with the brilliance and grit to work through your area of stuckness, the one who fought off surges of self-doubt, the one who practiced the exercises, and the one who persisted in your efforts to change your life moving forward for good. *You are amazing.*

Life is unpredictable, and challenges will always lie ahead. But you are so capable, and are now armed with the tools and resources to surge forward within your desired state and maintain your trajectory. Revisit the sections and exercises of this book that really spoke to you whenever you need reinforcement. Conduct regular internal assessments before things don't feel solid in order to shore up your strength. Bring in huge doses of resilience, optimism, wellness, gratitude, and support to help you thrive as much as possible. Pivot whenever you feel a need to.

You deserve to stay unstuck and live the best version of your life. Congratulations for recognizing that, and for bringing so much positivity into your world.

And . . . thank you for allowing me to be part of your transformation.

ACKNOWLEDGMENTS

I'M ALL ABOUT practicing what I preach. Considering that gratitude got its own chapter in *Free and Clear*, I'm excited to recognize all of the terrific people who supported and contributed to this project over the years.

For starters, a big thanks to the one hundred-plus individuals who shared their stories with me. Your insights helped me identify and define the 7 Things That Get People Stuck. Although there are too many to list individually, I wanted to recognize certain people whose inspiring personal experiences became pivotal within the content of this book: Philippe Danielides, Marie Incontrera, Emeka Nwosu, Richard Bistrong, Patrice Tanaka, Misty Boachie, Laurie Arron, Moe Mitchell, Alyson Gondek, McClain Hermes, Ann Dowsett Johnston, Jenny Lisk, Qing Li, Anne Buckingham, Meredith Moore, Suzanne Case, Ali Davies, Abby Maxman, Spencer Koeneman, and Jennifer Nash, PhD.

Also, I'd like to thank the brilliant subject-matter experts who generously shared their expertise with me, often during multiple conversations, throughout this process: Lisa Ferentz, LCSW-C DAPA; Kristina Hallett, PhD; Susannah Chambers; Richard Shuster, PhD; Dorie Clark; Lisa DeAngelis, PhD; Rachael O'Meara; Kacey Cardin, ACCC, PCC; Jon DeWaal; Tammy Gooler Loeb, CPCC; Ludmila N. Praslova, PhD; Monique Russell; Samantha Fowlds; Nancy Taylor; Andy Molinsky, PhD; Brenda Bence; S. D. Shanti, DDS, PhD; Sherri W. Fisher; Barbara Fagan-Smith; Anda Goseco, ICF-PCC; and Inga Chamberlain, PhD. You rock.

I'm grateful for my fantastic editor, Jessica Easto, and the top-notch publishing team of Maggie Langrick and Allison Serrell at Wonderwell. None of this would have happened without huge support from great cheerleaders and mentors like Kenneth Carter, PhD, Caroline Stokes, Steve Gildersleeve, Amy Storey, Samantha Worthen, Michelle Goss, Deborah McCoy, Ginger Schlanger, Leigh Higginbotham, Sue Koeneman, Faye Miller, Rachel Kitchens, Anthony Surratt, and Ron Carucci.

And of course, I saved the best for last. Most of all, thanks to my amazing husband, Justin Mason. You are my favorite person ever, the source of so much goodness, and yes, it's apparent that you "do everything." I love you so much.

RESOURCES

Wheel of Life Chart* | Page 216

Grid of Values* | Page 217

Permission Slip | ShiraMiller.com/tools

VIA Character Strengths Survey & Character Reports | VIACharacter.org

CliftonStrengths Assessment | Gallup.com/cliftonstrengths

Note: These items can be downloaded at ShiraMiller.com/tools

Wheel of Life Chart

The ten sections in the wheel represent the major areas of life.

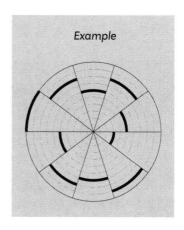
Example

Seeing the center of the wheel as a 0 and the outer edge as a 10, rank your level of *satisfaction* with each life area by drawing a curved line to create a new outer edge. The new perimeter of the circle represents your Wheel of Life at this point in time.

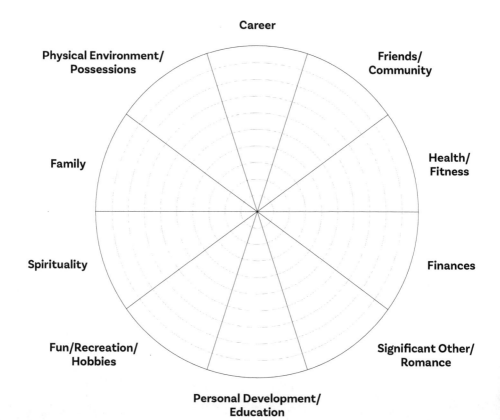

Identify Your Values

Understanding your values—the beliefs that guide your behavior and represent who you are at your core—can help you find your purpose. Review the grid of values below, circling any that resonate strongly with you. Then pinpoint your top-five values from your initial selection to gain deeper awareness about who you are. Don't see a value listed that is essential to your core? Add it to the chart so it can make your top choices.

Achievement	Ethics	Humor	Security
Adventure	Faith	Independence	Spirituality
Acceptance	Family	Innovation	Success
Ambition	Freedom	Intelligence	Tenacity
Altruism	Friends	Joy	Traditional
Compassion	Fun	Kindness	Wellness
Commitment	Gratitude	Love	Unconventional
Courage	Growth	Loyalty	Vigilance
Creativity	Happiness	Optimism	
Curiosity	Health	Prosperity	
Education	Honesty	Recognition	
Empathy	Hope	Reliability	
Equality	Humbleness	Resilience	

My top values:

1.
2.
3.
4.
5.

FURTHER READING

Atomic Habits: An Easy and Proven Way to Build Good Habits and Break Bad Ones by James Clear
Becoming Ginger Rogers: How Ballroom Dancing Made Me a Happier Woman, a Better Partner, and a Smarter CEO by Patrice Tanaka
The Best Place to Work: The Art and Science of Creating an Extraordinary Workplace by Ron Friedman
Daring Greatly: How the Courage to Be Vulnerable Transforms the Way We Live, Love, Parent, and Lead by Brené Brown
Drink: The Intimate Relationship Between Women and Alcohol by Ann Dowsett Johnston
The Effort Myth: How to Give Your Child the Gift of Motivation by Sherri W. Fisher
Elephants Before Unicorns: Emotionally Intelligent HR Strategies to Save Your Company by Caroline Stokes
Forgive for Good: A Proven Prescription for Health and Happiness by Frederic Luskin
The Forgotten Choice: Shift Your Inner Mindset, Shape Your Outer World by Brenda Bence
The Four Agreements: A Practical Guide to Personal Freedom by Don Miguel Ruiz
Future Widow: Losing My Husband, Saving My Family, and Finding My Voice by Jenny Lisk
Living ROI: A Weekly Guide for Soulful Living by Barbara Fagan-Smith

The Long Game: How to Be a Long-Term Thinker in a Short-Term World by Dorie Clark

The Path to Purpose: Helping Our Children Find Their Calling in Life by William Damon

Pause: Harnessing the Life-Changing Power of Giving Yourself a Break by Rachael O'Meara

Pivot: The Only Move That Matters Is Your Next One by Jenny Blake

Positive Intelligence by Shirzad Chamine

Reach: A New Strategy to Help You Step Outside Your Comfort Zone, Rise to the Challenge, and Build Confidence by Andy Molinsky, PhD

Self-Compassion: The Proven Power of Being Kind to Yourself by Kristin Neff

The Self-Confidence Workbook: A Guide to Overcoming Self-Doubt and Improving Self-Esteem by Barbara Markway

Start with Why: How Great Leaders Inspire Everyone to Take Action by Simon Sinek

The Tipping Point: How Little Things Can Make a Big Difference by Malcolm Gladwell

Thrive: The Third Metric to Redefining Success and Creating a Life of Well-Being, Wisdom, and Wonder by Arianna Huffington

Together Is Better: A Little Book of Inspiration by Simon Sinek

Work from the Inside Out: Break Through Nine Common Obstacles and Design a Career That Fulfills You by Tammy Gooler Loeb

ENDNOTES

Chapter 1

1. Jamie Ducharme, "Why the COVID-19 Pandemic Has Caused a Widespread Existential Crisis," *Time*, December 29, 2020, time.com/5925218/covid-19-pandemic-life-decisions.

Chapter 2

1. Jennifer Foust, "What It Means to Be Your Authentic Self?" Center for Growth, accessed October 21, 2020, thecenterforgrowth.com/tips/what-it-means-to-be-your-authentic-self.

2. Mel Schwartz, "Seeking Authenticity," *Psychology Today*, August 2, 2012, psychologytoday.com/us/blog/shift-mind/201208/seeking-authenticity.

3. Schwartz, "Seeking Authenticity."

4. Swen Heidenreich, "Health Risks of an Inauthentic Life: Here Is What You Need to Know and Do," LinkedIn, June 10, 2020, linkedin.com/pulse/health-risks-inauthentic-life-here-what-you-need-know-heidenreich.

5. Rebecca J. Erickson and Amy S. Wharton, "Inauthenticity and Depression: Assessing the Consequences of Interactive Service Work," *Work and Occupations* 23, no. 2 (May 1, 1997): 188–213, doi.org/10.1177/0730888497024002004.

6. Francesca Gino, Maryam Kouchaki, and Adam D. Galinsky, "The Moral Virtue of Authenticity: How Inauthenticity Produces Feelings of Immorality and Impurity," *Psychological Science* 26, no. 7 (May 11, 2015): 983–996, doi.org/10.1177/0956797615575277.

7. Larissa Rainey, "The Search for Purpose in Life: An Exploration of Purpose, the Search Process, and Purpose Anxiety," (PhD diss., University of Pennsylvania, 2014).

8. Amy Morin, "7 Tips for Finding Your Purpose in Life," Verywell Mind, last updated July 12, 2020, verywellmind.com/tips-for-finding-your-purpose-in-life-4164689.

9. "What Is Forgiveness?" *Greater Good* magazine, accessed December 7, 2021, greatergood.berkeley.edu/topic/forgiveness/definition.

10. "Forgiveness: Letting Go of Grudges and Bitterness," Mayo Clinic, November 13, 2020, mayoclinic.org/healthy-lifestyle/adult-health/in-depth/forgiveness/art-20047692.

11. Henrik Edberg, "76 Forgiveness Quotes for Letting Go of Hurt and Anger," *The Positivity Blog*, last updated October 5, 2021, positivityblog.com/10-inspirational-quotes-on-forgiveness.

12. Therese J. Borchard, "30 Healing Quotes on Self-Forgiveness," PsychCentral, February 3, 2019, psychcentral.com/blog/30-healing-quotes-on-self-forgiveness#3.

13. Everette L. Worthington Jr., "The New Science of Forgiveness," *Greater Good* magazine, September 1, 2004, greatergood.berkeley.edu/article/item/the_new_science_of_forgiveness.

14. Worthington, "The New Science of Forgiveness."

15. M.D. Braslow, J. Guerrettaz, R.M. Arkin, and K.C. Oleson, "Self-Doubt," *Social and Personality Psychology Compass* 6, no. 6 (May 31, 2012): 470–482, doi.org/10.1111/j.1751-9004.2012.00441.x.

16. Justin W. Peer and Pamela McAuslan, "Self-Doubt During Emerging Adulthood: The Conditional Mediating Influence of Mindfulness," *Emerging Adulthood* 4, no. 3 (April 9, 2015): 176–185, doi.org/10.1177/2167696815579828.

17. Sandra Silva Casabianca, "Stuck in the Negatives? 15 Cognitive Distortions to Blame," PsychCentral, May 6, 2021, psychcentral.com/lib/cognitive-distortions-negative-thinking#types.

18. Kendra Cherry, "How the Fight-or-Flight Response Works," Verywell Mind, last updated August 18, 2019, verywellmind.com/what-is-the-fight-or-flight-response-2795194.

19. "Understanding the Stress Response," Harvard Health, July 6, 2020, health.harvard.edu/staying-healthy/understanding-the-stress-response.

20. Mikko Pänkäläinen et al., "Pessimism and Risk of Death from Coronary Heart Disease Among Middle-Aged and Older Finns: An Eleven-Year Follow-Up Study," *BMC Public Health* 16, no. 1124 (2016), doi.org/10.1186/s12889-016-3764-8.

21. "Resilience," Psychology Today, accessed December 7, 2021, psychologytoday.com/us/basics/resilience.

22. "Resilience."

23. Jamie Ducharme, "The Sunk Cost Fallacy Is Ruining Your Decisions," *Time*, July 26, 2018, time.com/5347133/sunk-cost-fallacy-decisions.

24. Niloofar Tavakoli, Amanda Broyles, Erin K. Reid, J. Robert Sandoval, and Virmarie Correa-Fernández, "Psychological Inflexibility as It Relates to Stress, Worry, Generalized Anxiety, and Somatization in an Ethnically Diverse Sample of College Students," *Journal of Contextual Behavioral Science* 11 (January 2019): 1–5, doi.org/10.1016/j.jcbs.2018.11.001.

25. Tsukasa Kato, "Impact of Psychological Inflexibility on Depressive Symptoms and Sleep Difficulty in a Japanese Sample," *Springerplus* 5, no. 1 (June 14, 2016): 712, doi.org/10.1186/s40064-016-2393-0.

26. Chris Guillebeau, "What Makes a Community?," accessed December 7, 2021, chrisguillebeau.com/what-makes-a-community.

27. "Loneliness and Social Isolation Linked to Serious Health Conditions," CDC, last updated April 29, 2021, cdc.gov/aging/publications/features/lonely-older-adults.html.

28. "Isolation," GoodTherapy, last updated August 20, 2018, goodtherapy.org/learn-about-therapy/issues/isolation.

Chapter 3

1. Michael Blanding, "Psychology: Your Attention, Please," *Princeton Alumni Weekly*, June 3, 2015, paw.princeton.edu/article/psychology-your-attention-please.

2. Joseph R. Ferrari and Catherine A. Roster, "Delaying Disposing: Examining the Relationship between Procrastination and Clutter across Generations," *Current Psychology* 34 (2018): 426–431, doi.org/10.1007/s12144-017-9679-4.

3. Darby Saxbe and Rena L. Repetti, "For Better or Worse? Coregulation of Couples' Cortisol Levels and Mood States," *Journal of Personality and Social Psychology* 98, no. 1 (January 2010): 92–103, doi.org/10.1037/a0016959.

4. Silvia Bellezza, Neeru Paharia, and Anat Keinan, "Conspicuous Consumption of Time: When Busyness and Lack of Leisure Time Become a Status Symbol," *Journal of Consumer Research* 44, no. 1 (June 2017): 118–138, doi.org/10.1093/jcr/ucw076.

5. "Meditation: In Depth," National Center for Complementary and Integrative Health, last updated April 2016, nccih.nih.gov/health/meditation-in-depth.

Chapter 4

1. "How to Find Your Purpose in Life," Jack Canfield, accessed December 7, 2021, jackcanfield.com/blog/how-to-find-your-purpose-in-life.

2. Aliya Alimujiang et al., "Association Between Life Purpose and Mortality Among US Adults Older Than 50 Years," *JAMA Network Open* 2, no. 5 (May 2019), doi.org/10.1001/jamanetworkopen.2019.4270.

3. Dan Buettner, Blue Zones, accessed December 9, 2021, bluezones.com/dan-buettner.

4. Randy Cohen, Chirag Bavishi, and Alan Rozanski, "Purpose in Life and Its Relationship to All-Cause Mortality and Cardiovascular Events," *Psychosomatic Medicine* 78, no. 2 (February/March 2016): 122–133, doi.org/10.1097/PSY.0000000000000274.

5. Patricia A. Boyle, Aron S. Buchman, Lisa L. Barnes, and David A. Bennett, "Effect of a Purpose in Life on Risk of Incident Alzheimer Disease and Mild Cognitive Impairment in Community-Dwelling Older Persons," *Archives of General Psychiatry* 67, no. 3 (March 2010): 304–310, doi.org/10.1001/archgenpsychiatry.2009.208.

6. William Damon, *The Path to Purpose* (New York: Free Press, 2008).

Chapter 5

1. Brian Goldman and Michael Kernis, "The Role of Authenticity in Healthy Psychological Functioning and Subjective Well-Being," *American Psychotherapy Association* 5 (January 2002), researchgate.net/publication/251802973_The_role_of_authenticity_in_healthy_psychological_functioning_and_subjective_well-being.

Chapter 6

1. Yuet W. Cheung, Bong-Ho Mok, and Tak-Sing Cheung, "Personal Empowerment and Life Satisfaction among Self-Help Group Members in Hong Kong," *Small Group Research* 36, no. 3 (June 2015): 354–377, doi.org/10.1177/1046496404272510.

2. Cheung, Mok, and Cheung, "Personal Empowerment."

3. Aisha Beau, "A Beginner's Guide to Giving Yourself Permission," *Shine*, September 2, 2021, advice.theshineapp.com/articles/a-beginners-guide-to-giving-yourself-permission.

4. Hüseyin S. Yaratan and Rusen Yucesoylu, "Self-Esteem, Self-Concept, Self-Talk and Significant Others' Statements in Fifth Grade Students: Differences According to Gender and School Type," *Procedia: Social and Behavioral Sciences* 2, no. 2 (December 2010): 3506–3518, doi.org/10.1016/j.sbspro.2010.03.543.

5. David Cole et al., "Targeted Peer Victimization and the Construction of Positive and Negative Self-Cognitions: Connections to Depressive Symptoms in Children," *Journal of Clinical Child and Adolescent Psychology* 30, no. 3 (2010): 421–435, doi.org/10.1080/15374411003691776.

6. Elizabeth Scott, "The Toxic Effects of Negative Self-Talk," Verywell Mind, last updated February 25, 2020, verywellmind.com/negative-self-talk-and-how-it-affects-us-4161304.

7. Judy L. Van Raalte and Andrew Vincent, "Self-Talk in Sport and Performance," *Oxford Research Encyclopedia of Psychology* (March 2017), doi.org/10.1093/acrefore/9780190236557.013.157.

8. "How We Self-Sabotage," Positive Intelligence, accessed December 18, 2021, positiveintelligence.com/saboteurs.

Chapter 7

1. "The Connor-Davidson Resilience Scale," accessed November 3, 2021, connordavidson-resiliencescale.com/about.php.

2. Leslie Riopel, "Resilience Skills, Factors and Strategies of the Resilient Person," PositivePsychology, June 12, 2021, positivepsychology.com/resilience-skills.

3. Suniya S. Luthar, Dante Cicchetti, and Bronwyn Becker, "The Construct of Resilience: A Critical Evaluation and Guidelines for Future Work," *Child Development* 71, no. 3 (January 28, 2003): 543–562, doi.org/10.1111/1467-8624.00164.

4. John Fleming and Robert J. Ledogar, "Resilience, an Evolving Concept: A Review of Literature Relevant to Aboriginal Research," *Pimatisiwin: Journal of Aboriginal and Indigenous Community Health* 6, no. 2 (Summer 2008): 7–23, ncbi.nlm.nih.gov/pmc/articles/PMC2956753/.

5. Martin E.P. Seligman, "Building Resilience," *Harvard Business Review*, April 2011, hbr.org/2011/04/building-resilience.

6. Catherine Moore, "Learned Optimism: Is Martin Seligman's Glass Half Full?" Positive Psychology, accessed December 17, 2021, positivepsychology.com/learned-optimism.

7. Seligman, "Building Resilience."

8. Pooja Soni, "A Study on the Relationship Between Resilience and Forgiveness," *Indian Journal of Mental Health* 3, no. 1 (January 2015): 57, doi.org/10.30877/IJMH.3.1.2016.57-61.

9. Linda Cox Broyles, "Resilience: Its Relationship to Forgiveness in Older Adults University of Tennessee," (PhD diss., University of Tennessee, Knoxville, 2015).

10. Jamie D. Aten, "Resilience and Forgiveness," Psychology Today, January 8, 2019, psychologytoday.com/us/blog/heal-and-carry/201901/resilience-and-forgiveness.

11. Dolores Radding, "The Health Benefits of Forgiveness," Kaiser Permanente, December 15, 2017, lookinside.kaiserpermanente.org/health-benefits-forgiveness.

Chapter 8

1. "The Power of Positive Thinking," Johns Hopkins Medicine, accessed December 17, 2021, hopkinsmedicine.org/health/wellness-and-prevention/the-power-of-positive-thinking.

2. "The Power of Positive Thinking."

3. Eric S. Kim, Kaitlin A. Hagan, Francine Grodstein, Dawn L. DeMeo, Immaculata De Vivo, and Laura D. Kubzansky, "Optimism and Cause-Specific Mortality: A Prospective Cohort Study," *American Journal of Epidemiology* 185, no. 1 (January 2017): 21–29, doi.org/10.1093/aje/kww182.

4. Sarah Treleaven, "The Science Behind Happy Relationships," *Time*, June 26, 2018, time.com/5321262/science-behind-happy-healthy-relationships.

5. S.L. Gable and H.T. Reis, "Good News! Capitalizing on Positive Events in an Interpersonal Context," *Advances in Experimental Social Psychology* 42 (2010): 195–257, doi.org/10.1016/S0065-2601(10)42004-3.

6. Claire Eagleson, Sarra Hayes, Andrew Mathews, Gemma Perman, and Colette R. Hirscha, "The Power of Positive Thinking: Pathological Worry Is Reduced by Thought Replacement in Generalized Anxiety Disorder," *Behaviour Research and Therapy* 78 (March 2016): 13–18, doi.org/10.1016/j.brat.2015.12.017.

7. Annahita Varahrami, Randolph C. Arnau, David H. Rosen, and Nathan Mascaro, "The Relationships Between Meaning, Hope, and Psychosocial Development," *International Journal of Existential Psychology & Psychotherapy* 3, no. 1 (January 1, 2010), meaning.ca/ijepp-article/vol3-no1/the-relationships-between-meaning-hope-and-psychosocial-development.

8. Carol Dweck, "What Having a 'Growth Mindset' Actually Means," *Harvard Business Review*, January 13, 2016, hbr.org/2016/01/what-having-a-growth-mindset-actually-means.

9. Dweck, "What Having a 'Growth Mindset' Actually Means."

10. "3 Good Things: An Exercise to Boost Happiness," Mind Fuel Daily, accessed December 17, 2021, mindfueldaily.com/livewell/3-good-things-an-exercise-to-boost-happiness.

Chapter 9

1. Oliver Page, "How to Leave Your Comfort Zone and Enter Your Growth Zone," Positive Psychology, accessed December 18, 2021, positivepsychology.com/comfort-zone.

2. Shadé Zahrai, "4 Key Benefits to Stepping Outside Your Comfort Zone," Thrive Global, July 8, 2018, thriveglobal.com/stories/4-key-benefits-to-stepping-outside-your-comfort-zone.

Chapter 10

1. Fatih Ozbay, Douglas C. Johnson, Eleni Dimoulas, C.A. Morgan, Dennis Charney, and Steven Southwick, "Social Support and Resilience to Stress: From Neurobiology to Clinical Practice," *Psychiatry (Edgmont)* 4, no. 5 (May 2007): 35–40, ncbi.nlm.nih.gov/pmc/articles/PMC2921311/.

2. "Support Groups: Make Connections, Get Help," Mayo Clinic, August 29, 2020, mayoclinic.org/healthy-lifestyle/stress-management/in-depth/support-groups/art-20044655.

3. "Get Professional Help If You Need It," Mental Health America, accessed December 17, 2021, mhanational.org/get-professional-help-if-you-need-it.

4. Emmy E. Werner and Ruth S. Smith, "An Epidemiologic Perspective on Some Antecedents and Consequences of Childhood Mental Health Problems and Learning Disabilities: A Report from the Kauai Longitudinal Study," *Journal of the American Academy of Child Psychiatry* 18, no. 2 (Spring 1979): 292–306, jaacap.org/action/showPdf?pii=S0002-7138%2809%2961044-X.

5. Liz Mineo, "Good Genes Are Nice, but Joy Is Better," *Harvard Gazette*, April 11, 2017, news.harvard.edu/gazette/story/2017/04/over-nearly-80-years-harvard-study-has-been-showing-how-to-live-a-healthy-and-happy-life/.

6. Tristen K. Inagaki, Kate E. Bryne Haltom, Shosuke Suzuki, Ivana Jevtic, Erica Hornstein, Julienne E. Bower, and Naomi I. Eisenberger, "The Neurobiology of Giving Versus Receiving Support: The Role of Stress-Related and Social Reward–Related Neural Activity," *Psychosomatic Medicine* 78, no. 4 (May 2016): 443–453, doi.org/10.1097/PSY.0000000000000302.

Chapter 11

1. "What Is Wellness?" Global Wellness Institute, accessed December 17, 2021, globalwellnessinstitute.org/what-is-wellness.

2. "Keys to Well-Being," *Greater Good* magazine, accessed December 18, 2021, greatergood.berkeley.edu/key.

3. Jeremy Adam Smith, "The Benefits of Feeling Awe," *Greater Good* magazine, May 30, 2016, greatergood.berkeley.edu/article/item/the_benefits_of_feeling_awe.

4. "Quizzes," *Greater Good* magazine, accessed December 18, 2021, greatergood.berkeley.edu/quizzes.

5. "Exercise: 7 Benefits of Regular Physical Activity," Mayo Clinic, October 8, 2021, mayoclinic.org/healthy-lifestyle/fitness/in-depth/exercise/art-20048389.

6. Ron Friedman, "Regular Exercise Is Part of Your Job," *Harvard Business Review*, October 03, 2014, hbr.org/2014/10/regular-exercise-is-part-of-your-job.

7. Seanna E. McMartin, Felice N. Jacka, and Ian Colman, "The Association Between Fruit and Vegetable Consumption and Mental Health Disorders: Evidence from Five Waves of a National Survey of Canadians," *Preventive Medicine* 56, no. 3–4 (March–April 2013): 225–230, doi.org/10.1016/j.ypmed.2012.12.016.

8. Bonnie A. White, Caroline C. Horwath, and Tamlin S. Conner, "Many Apples a Day Keep the Blues Away—Daily Experiences of Negative and Positive Affect and Food Consumption in Young Adults," *British Journal of Health Psychology* (January 24, 2013), doi.org/10.1111/bjhp.12021.

9. "1 in 3 Adults Don't Get Enough Sleep," Centers for Disease Control, February 18, 2016, cdc.gov/media/releases/2016/p0215-enough-sleep.html.

10. "Why Is Getting Enough Sleep Important?" My Health Finder, July 8, 2021, health.gov/myhealthfinder/topics/everyday-healthy-living/mental-health-and-relationships/get-enough-sleep.

11. A.M. Williamson and Anne-Marie Feyer, "Moderate Sleep Deprivation Produces Impairments in Cognitive and Motor Performance Equivalent to Legally Prescribed Levels of Alcohol Intoxication," *Occupational & Environmental Medicine* 57, no. 10 (October 1, 2000), dx.doi.org/10.1136/oem.57.10.649.

12. "About MARC," UCLA Mindful Awareness Research Center, accessed December 8, 2021, uclahealth.org/marc/about-marc.

13. Richard J. Davidson, "The Four Keys to Well-Being," *Greater Good* magazine, March 21, 2016, greatergood.berkeley.edu/article/item/the_four_keys_to_well_being.

Chapter 12

1. Phillippa Lally, Cornelia H.M. van Jaarsveld, Henry W.W. Potts, and Jane Wardle, "How Are Habits Formed: Modelling Habit Formation in the Real World," *European Journal of Social Psychology* 40, no. 6 (October 2010): 998–1009, doi.org/10.1002/ejsp.674.

2. Lally, van Jaarsveld, Potts, and Wardle, "How Are Habits Formed."

3. "Journaling for Mental Health," University of Rochester Medical Center, accessed December 18, 2021, urmc.rochester.edu/encyclopedia/content.aspx?ContentID=4552&ContentTypeID=1.

4. Rebecca Kochenderfer, "Expressive Writing: A Tool for Transformation, with James Pennebaker, PhD," Journaling.com, August 8, 2019, journaling.com/articles/expressive-writing-a-tool-for-transformation-with-dr-james-pennebaker-ph-d/.

5. Kochenderfer, "Expressive Writing."

6. Shilagh A. Mirgain and Janice Singles, "Therapeutic Journaling," VA Office of Patient Centered Care and Cultural Transformation, 2016, va.gov/WHOLEHEALTHLIBRARY/docs/Therapeutic-Journaling.pdf.

7. Chad A. Buck, "Establishing Effective Personal Boundaries," Vanderbilt University Medical Center, accessed December 8, 2021, vumc.org/health-wellness/news-resource-articles/establishing-effective-personal-boundaries.

Chapter 13

1. "Gratitude Is Good Medicine," UC Davis Health, November 25, 2015, health.ucdavis.edu/welcome/features/2015-2016/11/20151125_gratitude.html.

2. "Gratitude Is Good Medicine."

3. Eric Lindberg, "Practicing Gratitude Can Have Profound Health Benefits, USC Experts Say," USC News, November 25, 2019, news.usc.edu/163123/gratitude-health-research-thanksgiving-usc-experts.

4. Amy Morin, "7 Scientifically Proven Benefits of Gratitude," Psychology Today, April 3, 2015, psychologytoday.com/us/blog/what-mentally-strong-people-dont-do/201504/7-scientifically-proven-benefits-gratitude.

5. Todd B. Kashdan, Gitendra Uswatte, and Terri Julian, "Gratitude and Hedonic and Eudaimonic Well-Being in Vietnam War Veterans," *Behaviour Research and Therapy* 44, no. 2 (March 2006):177–199, doi.org/10.1016/j.brat.2005.01.005.

6. Lindberg, "Practicing Gratitude."

7. Paul J. Mills, Laura Redwine, Kathleen Wilson, Meredith A. Pung, Kelly Chinh, Barry H. Greenberg, Ottar Lunde, Alan Maisel, Ajit Raisinghani, Alex Wood, and Deepak Chopra, "The Role of Gratitude in Spiritual Well-Being in Asymptomatic Heart Failure Patients," *Spirituality in Clinical Practice* 2, no. 1 (2015): 5–17, doi.org/10.1037/scp0000050.

8. Adam M. Grant and Francesca Gino, "A Little Thanks Goes a Long Way: Explaining Why Gratitude Expressions Motivate Prosocial Behavior," *Journal of Personality and Social Psychology* 98, no. 6 (June 2010): 946–955, doi.org/10.1037/a0017935.

9. Grant and Gino, "A Little Thanks Goes a Long Way."

10. L.A. Williams and M.Y. Bartlett, "Warm Thanks: Gratitude Expression Facilitates Social Affiliation in New Relationships via Perceived Warmth," *Emotion* 15, no. 1 (2015): 1–5, doi.org/10.1037/emo0000017.

11. Tara Parker Pope, "The Science of Helping Out," *The New York Times*, updated May 6, 2020, nytimes.com/2020/04/09/well/mind/coronavirus-resilience-psychology-anxiety-stress-volunteering.html.

12. R.S. Sneed and S. Cohen, "A Prospective Study of Volunteerism and Hypertension Risk in Older Adults, *Psychology and Aging* 28, no. 2 (2013) 578–586, doi.org/10.1037/a0032718.

ABOUT THE AUTHOR

Shira Miller is a certified professional co-active coach (CPCC), an award-winning communications expert, and a two-time TEDx speaker who knows a lot about getting unstuck and emerging stronger and happier than before. She has contributed numerous articles to Medium and Thrive Global, Arianna Huffington's online community that helps people unlock their greatest potential. Her story and opinions have appeared in *Shape*, *Health*, *First for Women*, *PR Daily*, *Quick & Simple*, the *Atlanta Journal-Constitution*, *Emory Magazine*, and the popular podcast *Lifeology*. Miller also works as the chief communications officer of a $2 billion corporation.

If you'd like to continue the *Free and Clear* journey, please find Miller on social media @theshiramiller; or visit ShiraMiller.com, where you can receive her newsletter and share your inspiring journey.

Made in the USA
Columbia, SC
07 February 2023

11924814R00145